"*How To Be A Time Master* has a great mix of ideas and hundreds of practical tips that will offer something for everyone. It covers a huge range of activities that most of us undertake every day or week and offers great common sense ideas.
Robert Epstein, Head of Small Business Sales & Marketing, Microsoft (UK) Ltd

"A refreshing new look at an age old problem. The book explores the big picture avoiding the common trap of exploring time management in a vacuum. Perhaps more importantly it has lots of practical tips."
Simon Benn, Chief Executive, The Times 100

"Ian has provided a common sense approach to time management with his Time Lord Truths. The book is laid out in an easy to read format enabling you to dip into the areas that are a particular problem and deal with those first. Ian includes examples of common situations anyone in business will be familiar with and emphasises the importance of putting you and your family first. It's not about applying yet another time management system but using Ian's tips and suggestions to tackle the main problem areas and deal with the most important issues."
Clare Evans, Time Management Coach and author of *Time Management For Dummies*

"Effective time management is an essential life skill. Ian Cooper manages to drill down to the essen   d come up with simple to understand concepts
everyday personal and professional
Andrew Holroyd OBE, Past Presi

HOW TO BE
A TIME MASTER

HOW TO BE A TIME MASTER

650.1

MASTER YOUR TIME . . .
MASTER YOUR LIFE

IAN COOPER

CAPSTONE

This edition first published 2009
© 2009 Ian Cooper

Registered office

Capstone Publishing Ltd. (A Wiley Company), The Atrium, Southern Gate, Chichester,
West Sussex, PO19 8SQ, United Kingdom

For details of our global editorial offices, for customer services and for information about
how to apply for permission to reuse the copyright material in this book please see our
website at www.wiley.com.

Library of Congress Cataloguing-in-Publication Data   (to follow)

(ISBN) 978-1-906465-67-4

A catalogue record for this book is available from the British Library.

Set in 11 on 14 pt ACalsonPro-Regular by SNP Best-set Typesetter Ltd., Hong Kong
Printed in Great Britain by TJ International Ltd, Padstow, Cornwall

To Helene, for a lifetime of love, support and years of inspiration

CONTENTS

INTRODUCTION

You only have a certain number of minutes, hours, days, weeks, months and years. How you choose to spend them influences everything that happens to you.

How much time do you waste each day in useless meetings, on the end of a phone listening to recorded messages, standing in queues, waiting in traffic, sitting on a train, looking for things, reading useless and unwanted emails, getting interrupted, putting things off and battling pointless red tape?

If you could gain at least 24 extra minutes a day by avoiding these time traps, you would have gained 145.6 hours in a year, or six whole days. God made the world in six days and then had a day off. What could you achieve?

So who or what is a Time Master? The key word is *control*. A Time Master is someone who has mastered the art, the science and the practice of gaining better control over how they spend and manage their life in order to maximize their time. The simple truth is that if you're not in control of your time, other people and circumstances are. Work, friends, family, colleagues, businesses, public bodies and technology all conspire to drain you of your time – but only if you let them.

How to Be a Time Master challenges a number of preconceived notions, myths and traditional views on time management. In a down-to-earth, light, conversational, observational and practical way, it looks not only at some profound issues relating to time, but also at the mundane time traps of everyday life and how to minimize them.

From my research, reading and consultancy over 30 years, I can see that a major shortcoming in many books and courses on time management is that they want you to do everything at once and usually expect you to spend hours defining your life goals; working on expensive and rigid planning systems; creating and completing daily, weekly and monthly charts; clearing your clutter; and learning to do the hardest task first thing in the morning! It's no wonder some people are cynical about time management methods and throw in the towel after their first three days of filling in forms on their new 'time regime'.

In contrast, I don't expect you to start with hours of self-analysis about who you are and where you want to be in five years and I don't believe that one planning system, time management or prioritization method fits all. If you were going on a diet, you would want to find a method that fitted your personality and wouldn't realistically expect to lose all the weight in a day or a week. It's the same with time management issues. It has probably taken you a lifetime of inefficient and unconscious bad time habits and behaviours to achieve your current level of time chaos, disorganization and difficulties.

The good news, however, is that it isn't difficult to make a big difference through some small, simple, practical adjustments that suit your lifestyle and your personal time demands, without the irony of having to devote what little time you do have to wrestling with oversophisticated time management techniques.

In this book I take you through three general stages.

First, I establish what I call the Time Master Truths, a set of guiding principles that you should keep at the back of your mind. As you read these I hope you will recognize yourself in certain situations. These truths will provide the framework and foundation for much of the thinking behind the tips and ideas to come.

Secondly, I offer you a no-frills focus on your major time problems. My view is this: let's simply find the time issue that is causing the most pain for you at the moment and help reduce that. Once that starts to get better, move to the next area and so on.

Thirdly, the book is filled with over 400 practical time tips, pieces of advice and suggestions to help you take control and master your time. Some are in specific sections, while others are grouped together towards the end of the book. The range of issues they deal with is immense, including coping with email overload, dealing with television and Internet addiction, clearing your clutter, travelling, eating out, doing business and many, many others. The book is a treasure chest of practical time tips and you will almost certainly find some nuggets of real value to you.

To give you final food for thought, I have put my Time Master Commandments at the very end of the book. These are the overriding messages that you must grasp and act on if you want to be a Time Master.

Now, before you tell me how simple and obvious some of the material in this book is and that you already know some of its principles, let me say that I used to be very apologetic about their simplicity, until I asked myself an interesting question. If these simple time control and management issues are so obvious and basic, why is it that so few people use them and why are so many struggling with their personal time demons?

Success in becoming a Time Master is not a question of whether or not you already know these strategies, it is whether you can actually do these things and keep doing them – so the simpler the better.

Ian Cooper

beatimemaster@yahoo.com

www.beatimemaster.com

WHAT TYPE OF TIME MASTER ARE YOU?

Just how close are you to becoming a Time Master? Are you really as good or bad at controlling your time as you think you are? What are your key areas for improvement? Before going any further, learn the truth about yourself and find out now what kind of Time Master you are. Too busy? Make time. It won't take you more than nine minutes!

1. How do you plan your days?
   a. I don't have time to do any planning at all.
   b. I write down all the things that need to be done, prioritize them and then decide when they will get done.
   c. I think through my plan and what I am going to do and keep that in mind throughout the day.
   d. I put everything I need to do in a long list.

2. How do you choose what order to do things in?
   a. I don't analyse, I just get on with whatever pops into my mind first.

    b. I ask myself what the most important thing to do first is and do that, followed by the next most important.

    c. I always like to start with the thing that's most fun to get me going.

    d. I think it's best to get the biggest job out of the way first.

3. How often do you have to spend time looking for things?

    a. At least once a day – there's usually something I can't lay my hands on.

    b. Never – I like to have a place for everything.

    c. Several times a day – it absolutely drives me mad, I can never find anything.

    d. A couple of times a day – I often put things in a safe place, but can't remember exactly where.

4. If someone asks you to do something that clashes with something of yours, what do you do?

    a. Find a polite way of saying you can't.

    b. Tell them you'll see what you can do and let them know later.

    c. Immediately say, 'Of course, no problem,' and put off what you need to do for yourself.

    d. Find a way of doing both things even if it puts you under some pressure.

5. When people interrupt you at work or in the middle of a project, what do you do?

    a. Wave them in, feeling pleased to have a distraction.

b. Deal with whatever they want but feel annoyed that they have interrupted you.
c. Automatically tell them politely that you are busy and that they will have to come back later.
d. Find out what it is they want and then decide whether to deal with them or not.

6. **You are chatting with your spouse, partner or work colleague. In the middle of your conversation, the phone rings. What do you do?**
   a. Ignore it completely and keep talking.
   b. Answer it and have a conversation with whoever is calling.
   c. Answer it and say you can't talk now, but will get back to the caller.
   d. Know that you have voicemail set so that will take the call for you.

7. **You are in the middle of a task at home and have to walk through a room where the television is on, showing one of your favourite programmes. What do you do?**
   a. Pause and watch for a moment, then carry on with your task.
   b. Put the task off until later and sit down to watch the programme.
   c. Not pause or stop, knowing that you'll get sidetracked.
   d. Find a way of doing the task while you watch the television.

8. **You buy a novel to read. After 100 pages you decide you aren't enjoying it. What do you do?**
   a. Stop reading it altogether because you don't like it and find something you enjoy more.
   b. Plough through every page to the end because you don't want to waste the time you have already spent reading the first 100 pages.
   c. Skim read the rest of the book because it was expensive.
   d. Skip straight to the end to see how it ended.

9. **How often do you actively check your emails?**
   a. Every 5–10 minutes.
   b. I have regular or set times in the day when I check what has come in and stick to those.
   c. I'm very disciplined, I only look at my emails when I hear or see the 'ping' or message to tell me I have an email.
   d. I have decided to let them build up and check them once at the end of the week.

10. **How much time do you spend in an average week on quality personal or family activities?**
    a. Over 20 hours.
    b. Between 10 and 19 hours.
    c. Between five and nine hours.
    d. Less than five hours – I just never seem to have any time for myself.

11. Which of the following applies when it comes to estimating how long tasks will take?
   a. I generally underestimate how long things will take so that I always need extra time.
   b. Actually I don't think I estimate at all, I just get on with the task.
   c. I generally overestimate, meaning that I usually have time in hand.
   d. I am pretty much always right with my time estimates.

HOW TO SCORE YOURSELF

Simply look below to see how much you scored for each question, and add up your points:

Question 1	a) = 1	b) = 4	c) = 2	d) = 3
Question 2	a) = 1	b) = 4	c) = 2	d) = 3
Question 3	a) = 3	b) = 4	c) = 1	d) = 2
Question 4	a) = 4	b) = 3	c) = 1	d) = 2
Question 5	a) = 1	b) = 2	c) = 3	d) = 4
Question 6	a) = 3	b) = 1	c) = 2	d) = 4
Question 7	a) = 3	b) = 1	c) = 4	d) = 2
Question 8	a) = 4	b) = 1	c) = 2	d) = 3
Question 9	a) = 2	b) = 4	c) = 1	d) = 3
Question 10	a) = 4	b) = 3	c) = 2	d) = 1
Question 11	a) = 2	b) = 1	c) = 3	d) = 4

HOW DID YOU DO?

11–17 POINTS

You are a **Novice Time Master.** You have a fair way to go yet! Focus your attention on the areas where you dropped the most points. This book is going to make a really big difference.

18–26 POINTS

You are an **Apprentice Time Master**. You have already mastered some of the basics but have a way to go yet to make a difference. Keep reading.

27–33 POINTS

You are an **Assistant Time Master**. You are average in your Time Master thinking. This book can help you make improvements very quickly.

34–39 POINTS

You are a **Deputy Time Master**. Well done. You clearly have a real grasp of how to think, but you need to watch yourself in one or two key areas.

40–44 POINTS

You are a **Time Master**. Congratulations, but don't get complacent. Read this book to enhance and maintain your skills and thinking.

THE TIME MASTER TRUTHS

Your thinking, mindset, attitude and approach towards time management as a topic combine to play the biggest single part in influencing how successful you are at getting the results you desire.

Many people have preconceived, negative and incorrect notions about what time management is and the extent to which it touches their lives. Most people have read the odd article on the topic, heard a few tips here and there and been fed and mislead by various time management myths, lies and 'motivational guru' jargon!

I want to set the record straight and give you what I regard as my Time Master truths. Understand these, adjust your thinking appropriately and you can't help but see improvements...

YOU CAN DISCOVER YOUR INNER TIME MASTER

I have often heard people say, 'I am not into all this time management stuff,' or 'I don't go in for all those "to do" lists and charts.'

Let's just be clear, if you are alive, you *are* into time management. Do you qualify? You practise time management every single second of every day. Time management at its most basic consists of the thousands of choices you make about how you spend your time and what your priorities are.

> If you watch three soap operas each week you spend over 312 hours in TV 'soap land', which is more hours than many university students are expected to spend in lectures in an academic year!

Time management issues involve questions both big and small. Take a look at the questions below and then ask yourself again, 'Do I do time management?'

- What shall we do tonight?
- Do you want to watch the movie or the soap?
- Shall I take a college course?
- Will you be my wife and spend your life with me?
- Shall I have a lie in?
- What time shall I set the alarm for?
- Shall I take work home tonight?
- Shall I answer the phone or let it ring?
- Shall we go away for a week or 10 days?
- Shall I work on the report first or deal with my emails?
- Shall I go to the gym first thing in the morning or after work?

- Shall I go by car or train?
- Shall I play golf this weekend?

All these questions are time management questions. The one thing they all have in common is that the personal choices and priorities you fix and make, have an impact on how you invest and spend your time. Whether you like it or not you *are* a time manager, so you might as well do it effectively and wisely.

EVERYONE HAS A TIME PERSONALITY - TAKE RESPONSIBILITY FOR YOURS!

Everyone has a 'time personality'. In my view your relationship with time and any time management problems you experience are mostly down to your own personality, style, approach, focus, set of priorities and general state of mind. That is why it is so important to understand that no one time management system is right for everybody. It needs to be personality led and not systems led!

With this in mind, are you:

- A person who naturally does things fast or slow?
- A person who underestimates or overestimates how long jobs will take?
- A person who likes to prepare in advance or at the last minute?
- A person who usually arrives early or late?

- A person who thinks most about the past, present or future?
- A person who waits patiently and calmly or gets irritated and stressed?

Perhaps the most significant of these time personality questions is whether your thoughts dwell most in the past, the present or the future. It is essential to get the balance right. I am in no doubt that good past memories are important, as is planning ahead with positive and creative thoughts about the future. But if you want to know which 'time frame' to invest most of your quality energy in, the answer is simple: the present. Want to know why? Because it is what you spend your time on today that shapes and creates your future!

The very least you can do is to be aware of the fact that you have a 'time personality', identify what it is and *accept* some responsibility for those time problems that are triggered by it. You can then adopt personal strategies and solutions that reflect your personality best.

CHOOSE THE 'PAINKILLER' APPROACH TO TIME MANAGEMENT FIRST

A very common approach to time management is to plan your life in precise detail, define your future aspirations, goals and outcomes and generally beat yourself up about your life's mission before you can really get on top of your time management problems. I recently participated in a time management course that devoted four hours to these issues before addressing a single practical time management solution.

The theory goes that you can't prioritize your time on a day-to-day basis if you don't know where you are going and what it is you want to achieve in your life. While I absolutely agree with the notion of setting goals and creating your own special big picture, I simply don't believe that you need to *begin* with this in order to solve your time management issues. There is a huge difference between planning how you want to spend the next few years – strategic thinking about the 'meaning of your life' – and learning some simple tips, tricks, shortcuts and tools to deal with the painful symptoms of not being in control of your time on a daily basis.

The practical truth is that in most cases, people who are struggling with time problems are too busy and stressed simply coping with today to worry about their one-, three-, five- and ten-year plans. Sometimes you just need to identify the problem, see what is causing the pain and take a simple painkiller. Once you are pain free it is easier to create your future plan.

With this in mind, take the painkilling tips in this book first and then when you are feeling better, more able to cope and have the amount of time that you require, do your aspirational thinking and planning for the future.

CONTROL IS EVERYTHING – PLANNING IS CONTROL!

Are you the kind of person who is continually reacting to whatever chance things happen during your day?

You sit at your desk first thing in the morning to check your emails, before getting down to a proposal you have to get done sometime soon. As you are replying to an email, the phone rings. It's a customer. You have three minutes of small talk about the snowy weather before you get down to business. While you are talking on the phone a colleague walks in and mimes the question, 'Have you got a couple of minutes?' You smile, nod and wave him into a seat. You finish the call, but before you can see what he wants, your phone goes again. Your colleague whispers, 'I'll pop back later,' and leaves. You complete the call and, intrigued to know what your colleague wanted, you go in search of him. He is not at his desk, so you head to the office kitchen on your way back and grab a coffee.

By the time you get back, there are three messages on your desk to call various people and one from another colleague, who is wondering what progress you are making with that proposal. You decide to leave the call-backs until later so you can work on it. After five minutes of searching for an early draft, you eventually get started, when someone pops in and says, 'Sorry to disturb you, my printer has run out of ink, can I just print an urgent document off on yours for a moment?' You have only been in your office 20 minutes and your day is gathering pace but not really going anywhere!

Does any of this sound familiar? Are you out of control? Do you jump to everyone else's demands?

As I mentioned earlier, a Time Master is someone who has mastered the art, the science and the practice of gaining better control over how they spend and manage their life in order to maximize their time. The simple truth is that if you're not in control of your time, other people and circumstances are.

The key to gaining better control is *planning*. I'm not talking about heavy strategic mission and vision statements. Time planning is simply the process of thinking about what choices you are going to make about how you spend your time, in order to keep control and to accomplish whatever it is you *want* to do. We'll look later in detail at various models of planning for you to choose from.

For now, just remember to apply the 'control test' mentally as often as you can. It consists of two very simple questions: 'Who has or will have control over my time in this situation? Is it me or someone else?' If it is not you, then you need to consider or plan how you can regain control.

Have you ever heard yourself using the following expressions?

- Give me a call when you are ready.
- Let me know when you want to meet up.
- I don't mind whether you come to us or we travel to you.
- I'm clear all day, I can fit in with whatever you want.

Who do you think has control in these situations? Remember the Time Master Truth: control is everything – planning is control!

HEALTH MANAGEMENT IS ALSO TIME MANAGEMENT

Over the years, I have read pretty much all the major books on time management and I have *never* seen any mention of health-related issues, despite the fact that the healthier we are the more time we have on this planet. Is that a good enough reason to consider your health?

If you knew that by doing certain things you could potentially increase your life span by several years, why wouldn't you invest your time doing those things?

Couples without a television in their room spend twice as much time having sex!

Consider the following facts and figures. They may just give you the leverage and momentum to put controllable health issues high on your own priorities list:

* 90% of those who join health and fitness clubs stop going within the first 90 days.
* Research among 5000 middle-aged people showed that those who had moderate to high levels of activity lived 1.3 to 3.7 years longer than those who got little exercise.
* About 91 million working days per year, a third of all sick leave, are lost because of stress. Failure to cope because of too much to do and too little time is one of the biggest causes of stress!
* 40% of working people skip breakfast.
* 39% skip lunch.
* Of those who take a lunch break, 50% allow only 15 minutes or less.

Do you know the single biggest reason people give for not exercising and taking better care? Every single bit of research shows the same number one: 'I don't have the time, I'm too busy!' My question for you is, how can you make the time?

TIME CAN BE SPENT BUT NOT SAVED, SO BUDGET CAREFULLY

Benjamin Franklin once said, 'Time is money.' Ben was only half right. What he was doing was pointing out the strong relationship between the two and the extent to which in many situations time has a real commercial value. Where he was wrong, however, is that while you can spend *and* save money, you can only spend time!

Time is the only resource that is absolutely irreplaceable. The sad truth as far as your time is concerned is that a second gone is just that – you can never, ever get it back. Yes, you can potentially live longer by living more healthily, you can learn to 'control' your time in order to use it more effectively and you can reclaim time that you may be losing at the moment to a whole host of time traps. But the one important thing you can't do is accrue time past to use again later when it suits you better.

If you watch certain popular television dramas that run over several seasons, you can clock up over 150 hours a year watching each one – that's a total of 6.25 days!

So the choices you make over your time, the most valuable resource of all, deserve at the very least as much care and attention as your decisions over money. Many people employ personal financial managers and almost everyone considers the need to budget to make ends meet. How much thought do you put into investing wisely in your choices and priorities in order to seize control of your time and make it go as far as possible? It is too important an issue to neglect. Mastering your time *is* mastering your life!

PUT YOUR PERSONAL AND FAMILY LIFE FIRST

Much has been written over the years on 'life balance' and juggling your various commitments. Let me tell you where I stand on this.

Most people fit their personal lives around their work and professional obligations. In other words, what is left over after your job is regarded as 'free'. You get the 'leftovers', the scraps of time. Work and business are usually equated with what we '*have to*' get done, as opposed to those elements of our lives that focus on what we '*want to*' do.

In the last 20 years, working time has increased by 15% and leisure time has decreased by 33%.

I know many successful people who pride themselves on their time management prowess. They actively boast about the volume of hours they work, the number of meetings they attend, the massive amount of business projects they manage, the thousands of miles they travel each week for their job and how early they get up each day to arrive at the office before anyone else. They claim that this is all because they are wizards at time planning and time management.

The problem, however, is that most of the things they apply their time thinking skills to are business or job related; very little if any attention is actively given to the personal things they want to do. The truth is that around only 5% of people have a plan of action for their personal life.

Being a Time Master is about reversing the process – it's about *starting* time management planning with the personal, 'want-to-do' activities and then building work and professional matters around those.

THINKING ONLY IN HOUR AND HALF-HOUR TIME FRAMES LIMITS YOUR OPTIONS

This Time Master Truth is to do with your personal relationship with time and challenges the way you are unconsciously programmed to think about and use your time.

Let me explain by asking you a few questions:

- When you set your alarm for the morning, what time do you set it for?

- If you stay in hotels, what time do you ask reception for your wake-up call?
- When you make your evening social arrangements, what time do you typically make them for?
- When you arrange business meetings, what times crop up in your diary more than others?

In the majority of cases, I bet the answers to these questions are in hourly or half-hourly units of time.

Here's what I found when I interviewed reception and desk staff at major hotel chains about the wake-up call habits of their guests:

- 50% of all wake-up calls are fixed for the hour, e.g. 6, 7, 8 a.m.
- 40% of all wake-up calls are fixed on the half-hour, e.g. 6.30, 7.30, 8.30 a.m.
- 10% of all calls are fixed at other times, all of them at quarter-to or quarter-past time slots.

So 90% of people are woken up on the hour or half-hour.

Likewise, apart from certain jobs or professions, 90% of people fix their business, professional, social and personal arrangements for hour or half-hour time slots. Look in your diary or calendar now to see whether you fall into that category. The chances are that you will.

I believe that people are almost unconsciously programmed to think in hour and half-hour time blocks. Most people don't question this and many of you won't have even thought about it until you read about it just now! Many diaries are printed in this way, and I have even seen watches marked out with dashes for the hour and half-hours and small dots on the quarters, as if other time frames don't exist.

What this means in practice is that if you are one of the 90% of people who think and operate in this way, you are limiting yourself when arranging and planning things to the number of hour and half-hour units there are in the day or the particular section of the day you are dealing with. For example, if your business day begins at 9 a.m. and the morning lasts until 1 p.m., there are only four 'hour' slots for you to fix meetings in or eight 'half-hour' blocks available.

When you fix your meetings or commitments, how do you know how long they will take? In most cases you don't. Most people fix their meetings and engagements around the typical hour and half-hour blocks, with some sort of 'gut feel' estimation given their purpose, and then *make* the conversation and discussion fit the time frame they've already mentally allocated. When time gets tight, people speed up and cut out all but the essentials to get things done, ready for the next engagement.

If you are able to be actively flexible within a meeting or activity in order to fit a prearranged yet random time slot, then why not operate in the same way but within different blocks of time, for example 18, 20 or 25 minutes instead of 30? It's up to you. If you work in 20-minute slots, instead of looking down at your diary and seeing a potential of eight possible half-hour units in a half-day, you now have 12 slots to play with.

The aim is not to make you rush things, I simply want to alert you to the possibility that life and your day don't have to revolve around traditional whole and round time slots. By thinking outside these, you can create more options for yourself.

'SUNK TIME' HAS GONE WHATEVER YOU DO: DON'T GET TRAPPED BY IT!

Have you ever had situations where you have already invested or sunk so much of your time into something that you feel obligated to see it through, no matter how much more time is required? Let me give you some examples:

* You're on telephone hold to some huge organization, waiting to be put through to the first available agent. You have held for 12 minutes so you tell yourself, 'Given that I've already waited so long, it would be stupid to give up now.'
* You've watched the first half-hour of a TV programme that you aren't enjoying, but you watch the rest because you've already watched half of it.
* You're a university student who discovers that you hate the subject you've chosen during the first year of a three-year degree course, but decide to see the course through in order not to waste a whole year.

Here is what I want you to understand and remember. The fact that you have spent time doing something in the past doesn't justify doing the wrong things in the future! Past time is 'sunk time'. Regardless of what you do in the future, your past time has already gone. It would be an even bigger misuse of the time you have already invested to compound it by wasting even more.

SLOW DOWN - NOT EVERYTHING IS URGENT

Many people create time and stress problems for themselves because they react to everything life throws at them as if it were urgent. In truth, despite evidence and feelings to the contrary, very little is truly urgent.

I have seen people run from one end of their office or home and physically fling themselves to get to a ringing phone. I have been in cars driven by speeding maniacs to get to a destination in time to see the opening minutes of a sports event. I have seen business folk operate to vein-popping bursting point to get a document finished by a specific time. I am not saying that these things are not important, but I am saying that they are rarely urgent. There is a big difference.

If you want to know how to distinguish one from the other, ask yourself this: 'If I don't get to the phone, do, complete or meet a particular deadline or task, *so what*? What are the consequences? How long term or far reaching are they?' Urgent involves major, life-or-death consequences. How often have your time demands fallen into this category?

SPEND YOUR TIME WHERE IT WILL HAVE MOST IMPACT – UNDERSTAND THE 80/20 RULE

When you throw your full energies and time into a new business or work venture, or at home on some personal task or initiative, what percentage of the time you invest will actually produce the outcome you are looking for?

Let's face it, there will be elements of what you do that produce fewer results than others. Doesn't it make sense, therefore, to spend your time on those components that will give you the best outcome?

There is a principle that states that 80% of effects or results come from just 20% of causes or inputs. For those of you who haven't come across this pearl of wisdom before, it is known as the Pareto principle, named after an Italian economist who noted that 80% of all property in Italy was owned by just 20% of the population.

Look at the following examples to see where this principle applies in life generally:

- If you run a business, isn't it true that 80% of your revenue comes from just 20% of your customers?
- In your social and personal life, isn't 80% of your time spent with just 20% of the people you know?
- What about your shoes? Isn't it the case that you wear just 20% of them 80% of the time?
- If you're in sales, have you ever noticed that 20% of your leads and calls give you 80% of your sales, and the other 80% of

your customers give you the remaining 20% of your business?

- Have you noticed that 20% of your family and friends give you 80% of your headaches and problems?

Don't get too hung up on the precise statistics here. Some of these examples may well be out by a few percentage points here and there, but the principle remains valid.

From a time control and management point of view, the 80/20 rule is a Time Master Truth that you should keep in mind.

Identify which of your daily activities at work or at home give you the best results or outcomes and spend more of your time doing those.

MASTER YOUR HABITS...MASTER YOUR TIME!

Many people give priority to certain activities simply because they always have done! The problem is not the habit itself, but the fact that all too often the habit is a bad one. Don't confuse time management and prioritization with your normal routine.

I have often observed people as they start their working day. What do they do? Here are a few typical examples:

- Many have a coffee and read the paper for 10 minutes. Do you do this? Why? Is it to ease you into the day? Is it because this is a priority activity that has to be done right then? Is this a good or a bad habit? I am not saying that you should or you shouldn't do this, but if you just do it because you

always have, then examine whether this behaviour is a positive use of that early and fresh moment of the day.
* Many go through their post and emails. Why? Does this have to be done at that moment? What would happen if, like bestselling author Ken Follett, you got on with your immediate pressing things and left your post and emails until a set time in the day? In his case he told me it was after 4pm.

Question why do you do what you do and when you do it.

MAKE CREATIVE USE OF YOUR TIME

I once saw a television feature was about a man who wrapped raw steak in foil as he left work to drive home. He opened the bonnet of his car and put the package on his radiator, knowing that by the time he had been driving for a number of minutes the steak would be cooked from his engine heat! He was filmed taking his cooked steak out of the car and putting it straight onto the plates of potatoes and vegetables his wife had ready.

I'm not suggesting you use this rather bizarre time tip, but it is a great example of someone thinking about getting the most out of his time.

What ideas can you come up with? Let me know.

ACCEPT THAT YOU WILL NEVER GET EVERYTHING DONE

Many people live in a permanent state of anxiety because of everything they need to do and see a formal time management system as a way of bringing this to an end. This is a bit like walking towards the horizon and finding that you are no closer to it.

As one set of tasks gets done, there are always more things to do, more stuff piling into your office or home for you to organize and more ideas, opportunities and challenges that the universe hands you to deal with. That's life! The problem is that many people haven't yet worked out that they will never, ever get absolutely everything done, sorted and organized.

Do you ever go to bed at night feeling frustrated by the things you didn't get through? Stop. Beating yourself up trying to get everything done is a fool's errand. Ultimately, when the time comes for others to look back on your life, you'll be judged by what you have achieved rather than what you didn't accomplish.

WHAT ARE YOUR TIME PROBLEMS?

One of my initial aims is to help you identify the specific aspects of your life where lack of time control is the cause of most difficulty and pain. Having done this, I then want you to consider the easiest and best 'painkilling' solutions and start there.

A traditional model used by many authors in this field is to take 'time logging' as a starting point. At its simplest, this involves keeping detailed records over a sustained period of days or weeks in order to see precisely how much time you actually spend on various activities. You may have realized by now that I am too much of a pragmatist to recommend this approach!

From my experience, more often than not a hugely disproportionate amount of time is spent on understanding, setting up and then carrying out this time audit, for it to tell you what you already instinctively know. For example, I don't need to invest hours filling in time sheets to find out that I say 'yes' to people too often, or that I watch too much television. What matters are the solutions.

What I invite you to do instead is to engage in a quick bit of *honest self-analysis*. Read through some of the biggest time weaknesses, traps and problems identified and encountered by delegates at my various seminars, which are listed in no particular order, and then simply rank them in order of those that *you* perceive are *your* biggest time demons. Which are the top three problems, traps or weaknesses that you would like to reduce more than any others?

Don't beat yourself up over this! If there are three that stand out and you can't choose how to rank them, it really doesn't matter; those three will do to work on. If you really can't decide at all which ones are your biggest issues, then ask someone who knows you well to choose for you.

Having made your selections, tackle the top three first and gradually work through your issues and problems *one by one*. The list directs to the most immediately appropriate section of the book. You should also make a visit to the contents page, as you may find other areas that will be helpful for your specific issues. Only when you feel ready for the next three areas should you go through the exercise again.

Let me be clear on this. One of my concerns is that many other time management-related books leave the reader with an overview of a number of areas, but no personal strategy for where to begin in order to make a difference. I don't want or expect you to do everything in this book at once. Simply identify the main three problems for you and deal with them *one by one* using the tips and suggestions I give. The truth is that improvements in any one area may have a huge personal impact for you.

What are your big three?
These are the most often mentioned time traps, weaknesses
and problems. They are in no particular order. Identify your top
three and go to the relevant section for tips on what to do about
them.

- Not planning effectively   Page 33
- Not prioritizing   Page 54
- Being messy and disorganized at home   Page 60
  and at work
- Spending time looking for things   Page 60
- Putting things off   Page 82
- Underestimating how much time things   Page 90
  will take
- Being a slave to the telephone   Page 94
- Being put on 'call centre' hold   Page 94
- Playing 'telephone tag'   Page 94
- Email overload   Page 104
- Watching too much television   Page 113
- Attending meetings that waste my time   Page 121
- Endless interruptions   Page 130
- People stealing my time   Page 139
- Always saying 'yes' to people   Page 146
- Coping with my boss who overloads me   Page 152
- Not delegating enough   Page 159
- Not knowing how to charge for my time   Page 163
- Taking too much time making decisions   Page 169
- Overdoing things and making myself ill   Page 175
- Not knowing what to do with my time   Page 179

1

MASTER YOUR PLANNING

I regularly encounter people who tell me that time management is not for them because they don't like planning. If their perception of this discipline is spending hours sweating over daily, weekly and monthly charts and never being able to feel spontaneous, then I don't blame them for feeling that way. It wouldn't be for me either!

How you do it and the level of sophistication is absolutely up to you, but know this: *any planning system is better than none.* If you don't plan at all, you won't have control over your life and others will. If you don't have a method and a habit of planning, then get one!

With this in mind, here are the Time Master Planning Truths. These are a set of very simple guiding principles that apply in every situation regardless of the planning method you use or the complexity of your life.

PRIORITIZATION IS THE 'HOLY GRAIL' OF TIME PLANNING

One area on which all time management planning experts agree is the absolute importance of prioritizing. Ultimately, everything boils down to this. You choose what you spend your time on at any given moment. Make good choices and you are on your way to becoming a Time Master.

When you have a multitude of things to do both at work and in your personal life, the problem you are faced with is deciding what order to do things in. People who just 'do' without any thought – and this applies to many – are always at risk of losing control of their time, getting less done and being more stressed than people who have a conscious strategy behind their choices.

The big problem, however, is how to prioritize in order to choose one task or thing to do over the rest. See Chapter 2 for my thoughts and tips on this question.

DON'T BECOME A TIME PLANNING JUNKIE

Don't become a time planning junkie or a slave to time planning charts. This activity is not an end in itself. When the planning process starts to become so time consuming that you have no time left to do the things you are planning, then take my word for it, you have your priorities wrong!

I have read books that recommend two hours a day of time planning. I don't know about you, but I can think of many more things I would rather do than give up two hours every day just to plan! In fact, anyone who has two hours to devote to this task probably hasn't got much to do.

So how much planning should you be doing? You need to do enough to make a difference in your life and that's it. If you are spending more than 10 minutes a day on thinking and planning your time, that is probably too much.

Avoid becoming too obsessive or inflexible with your planning. Plans are there to help you live your life to the full, they are not an end in themselves. Planning every minute of your time can take the joy out of living. It is the equivalent of a wealthy person sitting at home all day counting their money and deciding precisely what they will buy instead of getting out there and enjoying it!

You shouldn't try to plan everything. Being spontaneous is a virtue and you can't put 'be spontaneous' in your diary for 7–8 p.m. every Thursday, as one person I came across used to do. That defeats the purpose!

Businesses should heed this advice too. Some organizations and their management take time planning far too far. I have over the years encountered companies who are quite prepared to take every key member away from their main duties for days at a time at the busiest and most commercially significant time of the year to engage in time planning exercises. Of course time planning is good business practice, but not if it stops you doing business.

NO ONE PLANNING SYSTEM FITS ALL

Some time management writers focus on a particular, almost mechanical system of time planning – usually one *they* have created – and push this to the exclusion of anything else. You often read, 'Such and such a system is state of the art and the only "proper" way to do your planning,' which leaves you feeling intellectually inadequate and useless if you can't understand the system or it doesn't work for you.

While I do have the Time Master 'www question' system as my personal guiding principle to *any* planning method (I'll tell you what this is shortly), I want to be blunt, open and pragmatic with you: no one system fits all. Too often the focus seems to be on the mechanics of a time planning system without the recognition that everyone is different and has their own 'time personality'.

What is important is to create a system that works for you. It doesn't matter what others say, how it conforms to the experts' perception of what is good or how simplistic it is. At the end of the day the only test is whether or not it is helping *you* get more control of your time to use as *you* want.

Arguing that there is only one way is a bit like saying there is only one weight loss system that works. Some people advocate counting calories, scoring points, eating meal replacement bars, weighing in every week, avoiding certain foods, or doing press-ups every morning before their six-mile jog! The reality is that they all work if carried out sensibly and on a sustained basis.

My time planning message is that planning should be personality and not systems led. Later in this chapter I will offer you a menu of different planning methods to consider. Some will appeal to you more than others. Try them out, mix and match until you have something that gives *you* the level of improved control that you are seeking.

UNDERSTAND THE TIME MASTER WWW QUESTION SYSTEM

I mentioned above my 'www question' approach to time planning as a guiding principle behind every time planning system. This couldn't be simpler. Stick to it and you won't go far wrong. Each 'w' stands for an important question:

W = *What* do you 'have to' and 'want to' get done?
W = *When* will you do it?
W = *Where* will you write this information down so that it is easily visible and accessible to remind you?

The answers to these three questions will give you everything you need to plan well. The rest is detail! Let's explore these a little further.

W = <u>WHAT</u> DO YOU 'HAVE TO' AND 'WANT TO' GET DONE?

The key tool for answering the '*what*' question is the 'to do' list.

'TO DO' LISTS

I have heard many people say that they don't like 'to do' lists. If you fall into that category, you have a problem because every planning system essentially starts with a 'to do' process. You can't think and organize your 'things to do' until you know what they are.

You may have a massive choice over how you divide up your things and where you write them down and store them, but all planning begins with the 'to do' list process. Don't ignore it altogether.

The humble 'to do' list itself comes in varying levels of simplicity and complexity and can be structured very differently. Which of these do you think might work for you?

Level 1: The basic 'to do' list

This is just the process of creating a written list of things that you need or want to do. It is writing down the answer to the simple question: What shall I do today, this week, month or year? Think of something you need or want to do, put it on the list and cross it off when you've done it. That's the process in a nutshell. It doesn't distinguish between any specific projects or activities, or anything else for that matter. You just dump everything onto one list. Planning done!

I have come across people who knock this approach to time management as being flawed because it is too simple. What nonsense! It may not be the best method for everyone, but it is only too basic if it doesn't give you the required result. I have encountered many people, some of whom are very bright and in senior business positions, who previously did absolutely no planning at all and found that the humble Level 1 'to do' list transformed their lives.

If you are starting from scratch, this may be a great place to start from before you work through the other levels as you try to improve.

Level 2: The prioritized 'to do' list

This kind of list involves doing everything in Level 1, but deciding once you have prepared your list what your priorities are and what order you will actually do things in.

As I mentioned before, how you decide on your priorities is a potentially huge issue and one that I deal with separately in the section 'Master Your Priorities', starting on page 54.

If you can prioritize, it will maximize your chances of ensuring that the most important things – those activities that will have the biggest impact for you – are dealt with first. Remember the 80/20 rule from the Time Master Truths? The idea is to spend your time where the effect will be greatest and where it will bring you closest to what you want to achieve.

You can physically highlight and identify your priorities on your 'to do' list in any way that works for you. Some people like to grade and mark them as A, B or C tasks, others 1, 2 or 3 and many visually sensitive people like to colour code them in some way with a highlighter pen. You choose.

Level 3: The prioritized, time-specified 'to do' list

Again you have a list with everything on it, but with this approach not only do you identify and record your priorities in some way, you also consciously ask in relation to each item: When precisely will I do it?

For most people, asking 'When?' and putting the answer somewhere in their planning system is the biggest factor of all in reducing stress in time management and I include myself in this category. There is nothing worse than carrying around a

huge and growing list of 'things to do' in your head, wondering
'How will I ever get through them?', 'How do I cope?' or 'Help!'

Nothing works better than putting all the tasks into a list,
sorting them into some priority order in terms of importance
to you and then deciding precisely when each will be done.
Once you have put an item into your diary or planning system,
you experience a sense of peace and relief, in the knowledge that
a particular thing will turn up to be dealt with at the allotted
time.

DIFFERENT TYPES OF 'TO DO' LISTS

In addition to the three levels of detail just explained, there are
a number of variations to the 'to do' list format that you might
want to consider and experiment with.

The project-specific 'to do' list

Depending on your lifestyle or your job, you might find it
helpful to draw up your list under different headings, with relevant 'to do' items under each of them. The headings might be
divided into clients, or other categories of your daily or weekly
commitments.

If you are an account manager at a PR or marketing company
and you look after three main clients, for example, you might
have a list of things to do under each client you handle. As a
teacher or lecturer, you might have a list of things to do under
different classes you take as headings, along with another one
for administrative duties. If you are self-employed running a
small business, you might have lists for new business, past

clients or customer activity, and one for administration and finance.

How can you divide up what you do? What are your main areas of focus?

This is the method I use at Level 3.

The activity-specific 'to do' list

This method is not divided into subjects or projects but specific types of activities, such as telephone calls you need to make or are planning to receive, emails to draft and send, meetings and proposals to write. Of course, this again can be drafted at Levels 1, 2 or 3 and in any written format to suit your personal preference.

Time section-specific 'to do' list

I have also adopted this approach many times over the years. It is a major plank of my Time Master thinking that you must feel you have the flexibility to adapt and alter your way of planning to the changing circumstances of your job, professional or personal commitments.

With this system you might decide to divide your day into three or four time segments and work only on certain types of projects or areas of activity in the appropriate time slot. Remember how your school days were typified by a timetable of subjects? Well, you might choose this as the basis for your time planning. You might divide your day into four 95-minute units, for example, with each block devoted to either a specific client or project or a set of activities like phone calls or meetings.

Another way of doing this is to take a day each week per project or activity. You might do all your finances and administration on a Friday, while Monday and Wednesday are devoted to meetings and new business activities, with Tuesday and Thursday focused entirely on client service activities. Obviously, what is possible depends entirely on your type of job or personal life.

W = WHEN WILL YOU DO IT?

How often have you said to yourself or someone else:

- We must get together sometime.
- I need to call that client to keep in touch.
- We must sort out our holiday this year.
- I need to get through 1000 sales calls.
- I want to get back to painting again.
- I must draft that report.
- I want to start going to the gym again.
- We must sort our finances out.
- I need to get our database in order.
- I really want to learn to play the piano.
- I must sort out the shed at the bottom of the garden.
- I must ring my sister for a chat.

There is one thing that you have to do that transforms the above wishes into reality. It is relatively simple. Let me coin a new phrase; you have to '*when*' it.

Next time you hear yourself saying 'I need or want to do such and such a thing,' or someone says 'We must do something,' ask 'When?' and put it in your diary or planning system right then. Only when you have asked this question and given it reality and certainty by writing it down do you make an agreement or commitment to yourself or others that it *will* happen.

With this in mind, here are a few tips.

PUT YOURSELF FIRST!

I have already mentioned in the Time Master Truths the absolute importance of putting yourself and your family first.

Most people plan their business or professional 'things to do' first and fit everything else around them. Being a Time Master is about taking control of your time so that you can do the things that you 'want' to do. *Focus on yourself and your family first.* It starts with you!

Imagine you are sitting with a calendar or diary in front of you showing the week, month or year at a time. The starting point to planning like a Time Master is to ask yourself *when* you are able to do certain things. I will list some of them as a guide in a moment. I can't emphasize the importance of this aspect enough. Many people say that putting yourself first is impossible. The truth is that it only seems impossible if it is something you have never done before.

Focus and point your mind totally at the question of when you *can* put the following in your plan. Make it a priority. Block out time slots for these categories. You might even choose to mark them in different colours.

Time planning time

Despite the obvious irony, you do need to build in slots for planning, you just don't need to spend hours on it.

Many people like to plan what they are going to do the following day at the end of each day, either before they leave work or before bed. Others prefer to do this process in the morning.

I won't sit on the fence here. My advice is to make planning your day the first thing you do each day, either at home or at work. Never just dive in. Even if you have prepared the night before, spare just a few minutes to review or plan the day ahead. The reason I believe it is better to do this first thing in the morning is because how you feel, your mood, state and a whole host of changeable external circumstances may have a bearing on the order in which you do things.

The same applies to forward planning. Write into your system when you will plan your week and month ahead. I suggest you find a slot at the end of the week, maybe on a Friday afternoon, when you can identify the things to be done next week, and also perhaps at the end of each month to think through the month to come. Regard this as an appointment with yourself. If you can't do it at that time, then like any other appointment you need to reschedule.

Thinking time

Almost every day I encounter business clients or delegates at my seminars and events who tell me they are on the go every second. They are usually very stressed, regularly taking work home and often missing key business opportunities. They are often too busy to be successful.

Build 'time out' into your schedule. In other words, allow a bit of time just to stop, take a breath, review what you are doing and why. Isn't it the case that some of your best ideas or solutions to problems have come when you were in that state of 'not doing things'?

Time off

Always have some time off and something in your diary or planner to look forward to. This might be a break at home to get some domestic things sorted, a weekend away, a holiday or some family event. We all need something to keep us going when things start to get tough and we get under pressure.

What things do you have in place that fall into this category? If the answer is nothing at the moment, create something and put it into your plan right now. Even if you don't know what you would do or where you will go, write down 'Time off'.

In my planner I have 'Time away' written in for several days immediately after I am scheduled to finish this book. It is my reward for the hours of work on it. I don't know where we will go yet, but it is built into my plan and getting closer every day. Even the discussions with my wife about where we might go or what we will do serve as a mental tonic. When other possible things arise to be done around that time, I say, 'I can't, I am away for a few days then. Let's arrange a different time.' In other words, I am fitting in other things around the things I absolutely want to do.

Exercise

What type of exercise do you do? If you do nothing, find two or three short slots each week when you can do something you enjoy. I don't mind what it is, whether it is walking the dog, swimming, lifting weights, playing tennis, doing sit-ups at home or playing with your skipping rope and yo-yo. Anything is better than nothing.

The reasons most people give for not doing more exercise are 'lack of time' and 'being too busy'. This is, in most cases, not the real truth. The sad fact for most people is that exercise is not a priority and it is not built into our plan on any regular basis. Be kind to yourself, put something in your diary *now*. Some people have said to me over the years, 'I have tried that and it didn't work, things cropped up and got in the way.'

Let me be blunt. If you have nothing in your plan for exercise, then guess what? It definitely won't happen at all. If you put something in, it will happen more often than it does at the moment. For example, I have it in my planner to swim three times a week on Monday, Wednesday and Friday mornings between 7.45 and 8.45 a.m. Of course unexpected things sometimes get in the way, but with this time slot built in as the norm I go out of my way to fit other things around this commitment.

Actually, as it is early Wednesday morning, I am going to stop for a while – I am off to the pool!

Getting organized time

Around your home, office or workplace, you will have a multitude of sorting, clearing and general organizational tasks. If you don't have a plan for when some of these will get done, there is a strong likelihood that they will simply get left and turn into an overwhelmingly large job and mess very quickly. In the chapter 'Master Your Stuff' on page 60 I address this whole important issue. If you are going to keep on top of this area of your life, it starts with this simple bit of planning to block out some organizational time.

Catch-up time
One thing we all know for sure is that new things will crop up during the week in terms of business or domestic issues, things to be read, emails and phone calls that need to be dealt with. Build into your planner one or more 'catch-up' slots and save up these things for then. You may even want to build in one slot a day.

Family things
Most of us have family commitments or wants. Whether it is taking your kids to scouts, piano lessons or just having dinner with your partner, plan it in. Write it into your system as if it were any other definite appointment.

At least once a week, on a Friday night, my whole family sits down to dinner together. Nothing messes with this. Why? Because that is what happens on Friday night and any other event that might arise has to fit in around it. That is what being a Time Master is all about.

Hobby or outside interest time
Most people have things they like to do or get involved with. This might range from playing golf to taking an evening class

in DIY, learning a language, volunteering to support a charity or being actively involved with the local religious community of your choice. Whatever it is, decide what you want to do and put it into your planner.

Now if you look back at your open diary or calendar and see the things you have written in and blocked out for planning, time off, catch-up, exercise, family and hobby and interest time, then what is left is now available for the 'have to' things. This is what I mean by putting yourself and your family first. If you can't manage slots for all these categories, just start with as many as you can.

PLAN FOR THE UNEXPECTED!

There is one thing you can expect with absolute certainty with any time planning you do. Every now and then, unexpected things will crop up and successfully knock you off your carefully planned day, week or project. Build into your planning system time to soak these things up. If they don't happen you will have extra time. If they do you will be able to cope!

SET TARGETS

The more specific you are with your planning the better. Targets can also be very helpful. For example, on one level I could write in my plan that I will work on the *Time Master* book on Monday. I could, however, be more specific and put in my plan that I will work on the 'Master Your Planning' chapter of the book on that day. To go one step further, if I were to set a target of 2000 words for that section between 1 p.m. and 4 p.m., I am much more likely to get it done than I would if I grabbed a bit of time here and there between other things. You tend to accomplish the things you target and focus on.

So if you are:

- An author, set a target of so many words per day.
- A sales person, so many calls a day.
- A decorator, so many rolls of paper to hang.
- A gardener, so many lawns to cut.
- A teacher, so many essays or books to mark.

Your targets start to become a habit and you will begin to get on top of your tasks.

W = WHERE WILL YOU WRITE THIS INFORMATION DOWN SO THAT IT IS EASILY VISIBLE AND ACCESSIBLE TO REMIND YOU?

This is where so many people come unstuck. They don't have a sustainable system or method for where to put the answers to the what and when questions. I don't mind whether it is on a wall planner, calendar, diary of any size, personal organizer, electronic notebook or a full-blown computer system. The only thing that counts is that you have your own answer to the 'Where?' question.

PLANNING SYSTEMS

Whatever kind of 'to do' list method you use and regardless of the level, you absolutely must have it all in one place, either on one piece of paper or accessible from one screen of activities on your computer. You don't want several lists floating about on your desk or in different parts of your technology solution.

Of course, the format can differ from one person to another according to your own style or personality.

For example, despite having experimented with a variety of so-called sophisticated time management software, I still prefer a 'pen and paper', manual 'to do' list. I guess it must be my age! At the moment my personal preference is to use an A4 sheet marked with the date at the top. As mentioned, I use the subject-specific method at Level 3. This is usually the left-hand page in an exercise book.

I divide the page into four equal sections with a heading in each of the quadrants. They relate to the four areas of my day that take most of my attention. I head one 'Speaking activities and consultancy', under which I list all those things I need or want to do that day relating to that aspect of my work. This may include phone calls and emails with potential clients about in-house seminar engagements, talks or courses I have to prepare, arranging travel details and so on. Another is headed 'Author and book things', the third is headed with the name of the training company that I own and run. The last quadrant is headed 'Personal and administration'. I include in this list the many day-to-day administrative items of a personal or business nature that need my attention. This is also where some of those personal 'want to do' things mentioned earlier live.

In conjunction with my diary or calendar, I write up first thing each day all the things I can think of under their various subject-specific headings, identify and mark up which are the priority issues that absolutely have to be done that day, decide when they will be done and where necessary move some of them into other days.

By the way, I use the right-hand blank page of the A4 exercise book to scribble any notes, phone numbers, email addresses or ideas that arise that day while I'm wading through my 'to do' things. Because it's date specific, I can usually find any notes later with the minimum of effort.

Some people knock this approach, but that doesn't matter. It works for me. Being a Time Master is about finding and doing something that works for you and gives *you* control. When an approach stops doing its job, adapt it and find something else.

DIFFERENT TYPES OF PLANNERS, TOOLS AND METHODS

The purpose of this short section is simply to flag up the main attributes you should be looking for in planning tools and methods to help you answer the 'Where?' question. It is not my intention to review each method or product as if this were some sort of consumer or best-buy guide. There are simply too many products out there for me to do that. With this in mind, the main planning tools are:

- A standard diary
- A customized diary
- Calendars
- Year planner wall charts
- Pocket/portable electronic devices

- Software packages
- Your own personally developed method using a combination of the above

Whatever you choose, here are a few tips to bear in mind.

INVEST WISELY IN SOMETHING THAT IS GOOD QUALITY

There are hundreds of items to buy in the shops and online at a wide variety of prices. While you don't need to buy the most expensive – a leather-bound, gold-embossed diary still only includes the same number of days – nor should you get the absolute cheapest. Buy a cheap diary and you'll regret it halfway through the year when the pages start to fall out and you end up with Christmas Day on Easter Monday!

PUT EASE OF USE BEFORE FUNCTIONALITY

Over the years many people have proudly shown me the various software packages and electronic organizer planning system gizmos and gadgets they've acquired. They've bored me rigid as they run through all the things these can do. I have only once met someone who has actually mastered all the functions on his system: he had both a handheld device and a compatible software package on his desktop. The only problem is that he is almost always late for meetings with me. Perhaps he spends too much time playing with his toys!

EVERYTHING NEEDS TO BE TOGETHER OR ACCESSIBLE FROM ONE PLACE

I recently experimented with a new software-based time management system. It was great as a 'to do' list and it had all sorts of useful 'bells and whistles'. However, in no way did it link to a calendar function. One without the other makes something far less useful than a simple diary or wall planner.

BE CREATIVE

It is perfectly okay to develop your own method. If it works for you that is all that counts. You can create something that suits exactly what you want, or you can find a company online that will design and print a diary customized to your requirements. So if you wanted it to start from 1 April, have two pages a day but with the right-hand side blank apart from the date, that could easily be done.

BE DISCIPLINED ABOUT MOVING THINGS FROM ONE SYSTEM TO ANOTHER

How often have you been asked about your availability and had to say you don't know because your calendar is on your computer? Computerized systems can be great when you are in your office or happen to have your laptop in your jacket pocket! The problem is that you probably don't walk around with these things all the time.

The solution that most of us use is a diary, a pocket electronic device or a mobile phone with a diary function. This is fine provided that you are disciplined enough to keep the two things synchronized. Failing to do so spells disaster sooner or later. For this reason, one system, even if it's manual, is often better than two technological masterpieces.

2

MASTER YOUR PRIORITIES

Nothing is more important in your quest to become a Time Master than prioritizing wisely. In order to plan your time and projects to get maximum control, you need to continually make choices about what to do first and next, and where to spend your time to the best effect.

While this may seem obvious, even clichéd, my experience and observation indicate that only around 20% of the average work day is spent on valuable activities, while 80% is spent on things that have little or no value.

Some people wake up and launch themselves into their day at home, work or the office with no real plan or idea at all of what they will do. They live life by chance rather than by intent!

With these thoughts in mind, let me give you the absolute golden rule of prioritizing and time planning.

DO THE MOST IMPORTANT THING FIRST

Before you begin your day, a specific project, piece of work or indeed the planning process, you must consciously ask yourself this question: '*What is the most important thing to do first?*' Once you have an answer, that is what you should do. Once that is done, you move to the next most important task and so on. That way, when the day is done, if you haven't completed everything you've at least spent the bulk of your time on the things of most value.

Sounds logical and easy, doesn't it? The real problem and challenge, however, lie in trying to decide *what* the most important thing to do is. Most time management writers will tell you one of two things:

- Do the hardest thing first.
- Start with the thing that will bring you closer to your goal, assuming you know what that is.

I absolutely understand the logic of these two notions. I think they are both great pieces of advice and have no problem about inviting people to follow or choose one or other of them. However, I want to go a bit further in this book. Having talked to thousands of people in the course of my consultancy and seminar training work, the pragmatist in me tells me that there are also other possible issues, questions and approaches to consider.

I don't like or accept the idea that doing the hardest thing or the thing that brings you closest to your goal first is *always* going to be right for everyone. I believe that other issues are sometimes important and I want to encourage you to explore other possibilities and find a way that works for you.

What is important as far as I am concerned is not that you follow any one particular 'rule', but that you have a strategy and a *conscious* thought process that you can apply. Just stopping and asking key questions before you do anything is half the battle. Let me give you a list of possible criteria and questions to help you decide what the best use of your time is at any given moment, bearing in mind that both external and personal circumstances may change several times a day. When this happens you may need to re-evaluate what is most important, perhaps using different criteria and questions.

The reason I have put forward so many possible questions and criteria is to illustrate how complex this so-called simple approach is. The infinite variety of human circumstances means that we need to be continually alert to a range of possibilities and not stick rigidly to those that are put forward as being 'correct'. That is why I am not giving you a definitive Time Master rule or answer for deciding what is most important to you. Just make sure that you ask the right questions.

The truth is, I don't believe that you can create an objective framework for prioritizing, which is essentially a subjective issue.

Let me give you an example. My son, a final-year university student, was home for Christmas and had two essays to write with the same deadline. One was on a topic that he really liked, understood and felt confident about, while the other was on a subject that didn't 'turn him on' at all. Which should he do first?

Following the theory that is most commonly put forward, he should have started with the toughest one first and got it out of the way. However, he offered the following reasons for choosing the easier one first: 'I want to start with what I like doing, as it will put me in a better frame of mind for doing the one I don't like. I want to start that one feeling positive and confident, like I actually know how to write a decent essay. Also I know that if I leave the other one until it gets closer to the deadline, the pressure will motivate me to get it done and to bring out the best in me.'

He chose to start with the easier one. This got him in the best state for the so-called tougher one. He completed and submitted them both within the deadline and got great results for both. What would have happened if he had done it the other way round?

I have two other general thoughts that I want to share with you on this subject of prioritizing.

Make Time for the Things You Want To Do
Too many people are time victims. In other words, they spend huge amounts of time feeling resentful that they are doing things they don't really want to do, typically making the excuse that they don't have the time to do what they really want!

It is your personal duty as a Time Master to *make* time for the things you want to do. These must take priority.

Don't Worry About Unimportant Things

Many of us spend a massive amount of time in a state of anxiety, stressing and getting upset over things, arguing with other people or struggling inside with emotional turmoil over a whole range of issues and minor decisions. Did something upset you last week that you spent time on? What about the week before? Can you even remember now what it was?

When you find yourself getting churned up because of something that's been said, or because you can't make your mind up over something, ask yourself this question: 'Will it be of any real consequence in a year, a month or even tomorrow?' If the answer is 'no', it's best to just let it go.

That doesn't mean that you have to allow yourself to be trampled all over or do things without real thought, but keeping a sense of perspective is also a time management issue. Spending a disproportionate amount of time worrying about things of no real substance or consequence is a costly time trap and a mistake.

Questions for deciding what is most important

- Which is the most unpleasant or toughest task, so that you get that out of the way first?
- Which is the easiest and quickest?
- Which can you do that will put yourself in the most confident and positive state of mind to tackle the other things?

- Which will make the biggest and most profound effect on your ultimate objective?
- Which just 'feels' like the one to start with?
- Which issue on the list is giving you the most anxiety or stress when you think about it?
- Which task, if it had to, could wait until tomorrow?
- Which choice might have an effect on other people?
- What is most fun; the thing that you have been looking forward to doing?
- Which of the tasks has the most pressing deadline?
- What state of mind, mood or health do you need to be in to get certain things done?
- What actual time makes the most sense to do specific things?
- If something unexpected were to crop up, which task couldn't wait?
- Which will, when you do the task, make a difference to the outcome and result?
- Focus your mind on each and ask: what would the consequence be of not doing that particular thing today?

3

MASTER YOUR STUFF

My wife and I have some friends who are truly organized. If organization were an Olympic event they would be multiple gold medallists. Clutter, mess and chaos are simply not in their vocabulary or their life. Ask them about a trip they took four years ago and within seconds they can effortlessly produce details of restaurants they ate in and leaflets describing local places of interest. In the summer not a blade of grass is allowed to stray beyond its permitted length or borders. They are truly fantastic, I like and admire them tremendously and most importantly, they are very, very, very rare! Most people are not like this at all.

The truth is that the vast majority of people don't live like these paragons of organizational virtue. Some folk don't even know how disorganized they are, because after a while the mess becomes invisible to them and they haven't processed just how damaging and costly this state is in terms of their time.

Think for a moment. How much time a day, week or month do you spend looking for things?

> An average of just 10 minutes a day is well over *2.5* days of your time wasted over a year!

Let me put you to the test. Can you lay your hands right now on the following items at home or at work?

- An important file that you worked on three weeks ago?
- The business card of someone you met at an event last year?
- The padlock for your bike that you haven't ridden for six months?
- The slip of paper containing your various cryptic security passwords?
- Your passport?
- The new address of an old friend you want to send a greetings card to?
- The phone number of a business prospect that you scribbled down at a recent social function?
- Your telephone charger?
- Spare batteries for your camera?
- Your camera?
- Your birth certificate?
- Your swimming goggles?
- Your shopping list?

How many of these items could you go to immediately?

If you answered 'no' to any of these things, then you are at risk of disorganization.

To some people, being neat, sorted, well organized and knowing where things are is a sign of obsessive behaviour, weakness and dullness. There is even a fridge magnet reading, 'Dull people have tidy homes.' Amusing, but nonsense!

Most people don't get themselves fully organized because things have got into such a mess that they simply can't face the task and don't have enough time to sort things out.

However often time management, organizational and planning gurus blandly repeat their mantra of, 'You must get organized,' saying so doesn't get you the time, system or leverage to do it.

CREATING LEVERAGE

What do I mean by leverage? The truth is that people do things for one of two reasons: either to avoid something negative in their life or to create something for themselves that is positive. Until you have sufficient leverage – gain or pain – to get things sorted and organized, you won't find or make the time. Let's look at some examples.

SELLING YOUR HOME

I know people who have lived with mess for years but then decide that they need to move. The first thing they do to make the place look acceptable to potential purchasers is to sort things out. The prospect of getting a customer gives them a potential gain and becomes a huge lever. Ironically for some, once the sorting is done they decide they like their own home so much that they decide to stay!

SOCIAL VISITORS AND GUESTS

Personal and domestic embarrassment is a great example of this principle. Have you ever had friends or visitors coming to your home and you wanted to make a good impression? What do you do? Out comes the vacuum cleaner, you dust and polish and sometimes even chuck piles of stuff into cupboards, hiding it out of the way to pretend that things are tidy. Again, this is a powerful example of leverage. If it sounds familiar and this is what it takes, do you know what to do? Invite lots of people over on a regular basis! Maybe this will act as a prompt to help you get properly organized.

THE COSTS OF TIME, MONEY, STRESS AND PHYSICAL HASSLE

What does it cost in terms of stress, time, money and physical hassle to be disorganized and in a mess? Have you ever had to buy something that you already have but couldn't find? Have you ever been almost at screaming pitch because you're stressed out just looking at the mess in front of you? Have you ever tripped over something left lying around and hurt yourself?

Exactly how much pain, time, money or embarrassment will it take to influence you to get on top of your disorganization? If you don't do it now, what will your cluttered desk, office, home and life look like in six months, a year, or even in five years? How much will it have cost you by then?

The truth is that by investing a certain amount of time in planning and organization in a controlled, systematic and structured way, you will minimize these various costs and save a much greater amount of time from being lost in the future. This is your 'time profit'.

If you keep saying you haven't got the time, think of the story of the carpenter who had to saw 100 planks of wood in half. The problem was that his saw was blunt and it was taking him ages to cut each piece. A friend suggested that he get the saw sharpened. 'I don't have time,' he replied. 'I have to cut all this wood by the end of the day!' Is this you?

Let's look at how you can get organized without giving up everything else to do it.

ORGANIZATIONAL RULES

You need to understand a number of simple rules, phases and questions in order to organize like a Time Master.

PLAN HOW MUCH TIME YOU WANT TO INVEST

You don't need to blitz everything in one session. Often, as I mentioned earlier, the mere size and thought of the task ahead are enough to put you off altogether. What I want you to do is to 'pay' for your organization by personal 'time instalments' in order to make your investment easier to manage. To buy a house or a car, many people who don't have the money in one lump sum take out a mortgage or loan and pay it off bit by bit. Even large and successful businesses require credit to function. They plan to pay back what they owe in a controlled way that fits in with their own strategy. Likewise, what you need to do is to decide how much time you want to budget for in order to get really sorted out, and then plan to invest this time over a sustained and controlled period.

Are you prepared to invest 15 minutes a day, half an hour or an hour a week, or longer? There is no right or wrong. It may depend on your level of leverage! Any extra time that you put into this process may be more than at present and therefore represents progress.

PLAN WHEN

Having decided how much time you are prepared to budget for and spend to go through this organizational process, actually write into your diary or calendar system *precisely* when you are going to do it. It isn't enough to say to yourself, 'I don't mind spending half an hour a couple of times a week.' The act of writing it in and almost making an appointment with yourself makes it more powerful and valid. You have now made a commitment.

For example, if you have decided that you can afford to spend 15 minutes three times a week, choose what days and times are going to become your slots for mastering your stuff.

PRIORITIZE

The final thing you need to do in the organizational planning process is to decide exactly what needs doing in priority order and then also write this into your diary or time planner, alongside the time slots you have built in. This might seem like a statement of the obvious, but you'd be surprised how many people start sorting things out with no real structure or purpose. Typically, they end up with a bigger mess and can't face it any more. Clearly everyone's priorities are different, but look at those areas of organizational chaos that are causing the most pain or where you can get the greatest immediate gain. You might want a clear loft, but if your desk and home office mess is becoming costly because you are regularly losing important memos and missing appointments, then start there.

For example, instead of putting 'Organize' into your system on Monday, Wednesday and Friday evenings, 6.30–7 p.m., you need to specify precisely what your task is for each time slot. Alternatively, you might decide that something is a big enough priority to devote an entire weekend to.

Taking this notion of planning bit by bit one stage further, each particular job can also be broken down into pieces. So it is helpful to be specific and write into your plan Monday 6.30–7 p.m., 'Clear top of desk,' Wednesday 6.30–7 p.m., 'Sort top left-hand drawer'.

Every single job can be broken down into phases and it helps to see it this way. So clearing a garage that is heaving with stuff can be broken down into the four corners, or different shelves. If you're organizing over an entire weekend session, plan which elements of your job will be done at what stages over the two days.

DELEGATE

Ask yourself who else you can get to carry out certain tasks. Regardless of whether you are sorting your workplace or your home, the likelihood is that sometimes other people will be more appropriate for certain tasks. Identify them and get them on board, with time slots in their diary or planner too.

PREPARE

One chicken-and-egg dilemma is rarely acknowledged when it comes to getting organized at home or at work. As part of the organizational process, you will undoubtedly come across things that need to be put somewhere. However, if all your places are already full of stuff, you have nowhere to put them.

The starting point is to prepare by creating a system for yourself, so that you can get on with the job. This is no different from many other tasks that require certain preparatory work and the right tools.

PREPARE A PLACE FOR DOCUMENTS AND PAPERWORK

If you don't have filing space at the moment, you absolutely *must* create something. Regardless of who you are, how complex or simple your life is, whether you are organizing your personal or your work life, everyone generates paperwork that needs to be retained. If you have space for proper filing drawers, that's great. If you are short of space or cash, all the major supermarkets and stationers stock cheap plastic filing containers. You should invest in as many of these as you need to suit your requirements.

They don't take up much space and can be kept on a shelf almost anywhere.

Before you start the process of sorting out your stuff, divide and label your filing containers with appropriate general and then specific projects. Consider colour coding for certain general categories, for example material relating to different members of your family, personal finance, holidays, home maintenance and so on.

PREPARE A PLACE FOR TIME-RELATED PHYSICAL THINGS YOU NEED IN THE FUTURE

You have tickets for the theatre on the 23rd of the month, the post has arrived with your train tickets for the 27th and you have just printed off the route directions for your car journey on the 31st. What do you do with these various objects so that you can find them when you need them without wasting time?

As part of your organizational preparation you need to decide how you will manage these sorts of things. I have two simple suggestions.

A date-based filing system

Instead of a file drawer or filing container labelled according to topic or subject area, create *one* labelled with numbers representing each day of the month. When the kind of things mentioned above turn up, immediately put the items concerned into the corresponding number date. So your theatre tickets go into the slot marked 23, the train tickets into 27 and your route into 31. If your file container hasn't got enough slots, double up so that two numbers go on each label. Perhaps have a slot for future months too.

Use a pin board
Buy a simple pin board and stick it to your wall in the most sensible room. Divide it into several sections and label them according to whatever you need most. Tickets might be one heading and in that section of the pin board you pin your tickets. If you pin things up in the right place straight away, you will always be able to get at them.

PREPARE A PLACE FOR GENERAL STORAGE ITEMS
The sorts of things that I am talking about here are usually consumables, things that you need easy access to time and time again. From a work or personal point of view this could be pens, paper, print cartridges or batteries.

Simply select a drawer or sizeable container that can be kept on a shelf or in a cupboard, label it 'regular storage things' or any similar phrase that means the same thing, and put the items in there. The important point is that you only have one place for all of these types of items.

PREPARE A PLACE FOR UNREAD GENERAL INFORMATION
Most people manage to acquire and collect all sorts of informational items that they intend to read later. This might include newspapers and magazines or professional periodicals. How big is your pile? Have a tray for such items, but observe the following two rules:

- Be honest with yourself! If you are not going to read it all, then bin it immediately.
- If you do build up a pile of things to read in the future, at least once a week in your planned organizational time get rid of those things that you have either read or do not need.

PREPARE YOUR PERSONAL 'SEMI-AUTOMATIC DISPOSAL SYSTEM (SAD)'

The less technical among you may call these boxes or bags! Yes, this is really not brain surgery. You will need three reasonable-sized boxes or bags. They need to be labelled or coloured so that there is no confusion between them. One is for the things you want to 'Store', another for things to 'Action' and the last for the things you want to 'Dump'. I call this the SAD method of organization!

IMPLEMENTATION

So you have done your preparatory planning and you are ready. Now make organization work for you! Here is the simple organizational method that Time Masters use to master their stuff.

FOLLOW YOUR PLAN

If you have prepared as described above, at the appropriate time slot in your planner, take on your first challenge with your priority task. Only spend the allotted time on it and then *stop*. Aim to complete as much of the task in that time as possible.

Decide then and there what needs to be stored, actioned or dumped. If you are able within your organizational time to do the storing, actioning and dumping, then do so. If not, at the end of the session make your mind up to dispose of the items at your next session and write it into your planner. Aim to start each clearing session with three empty SAD boxes or bags.

REMEMBER, A BIT AT A TIME ONLY
If your planner says clear your desktop, focus exclusively on that. It is okay to ignore the rest of your office or study. Your sole job is the desktop and that's it.

It is important to keep in mind that you don't have rooms to sort, clear or organize, you have specific jobs in those rooms. For example, your kitchen list might have planned to tackle the left-hand cutlery drawer, the right-hand work surface, the crockery cupboard or the top bookshelf. Your bedroom plan might be broken down into your bedside table top, the second drawer down or the left-hand side of the wardrobe.

What is important is that each part becomes an end in itself for the SAD treatment, as explained above.

PERSEVERE
Everyone knows people (including ourselves) who start out on a new regime very well but can't sustain it. Think of those diets and weight loss efforts and resolutions. There are two main reasons people don't stick to them. First, many have unrealistic expectations and goals. They set out with the intention of losing 30 pounds in six weeks and when they see they are not going to get there, they become disheartened and give up, feeling a sense of failure. Secondly, they have no plan or structure

surrounding their efforts, so that the things that need to be done never become a habit or a matter of regular routine.

If you want to master your stuff, you need to set simple one-by-one tasks as described, one shelf at a time, so that you can always see and focus on something you have achieved. If you have planned in short, regular organizational sessions, those times also become a commitment and are habit forming.

MAINTAIN

Keeping things organized once you've finished the job is not always easy, but is a lot simpler than starting from scratch. The key is persistence and again, leverage. Is your life better in an organized state than it was before? If you want to keep on top of things, the system you have created needs to be one that makes it easy to maintain. For this reason, even when you think you are done with all your tasks, you should keep at least one organizational time slot in your diary or planner, in order to be able to keep things in an organized state.

COMMON ORGANIZATIONAL PROBLEMS AND QUESTIONS

Here are some of the most frequently asked questions and concerns about the methods I have just described.

WHAT IF THE ITEMS I WANT TO KEEP ARE TOO BIG OR BULKY FOR THE FILE OR STORAGE SYSTEM I HAVE?

Obviously, I can't tell you where in your home or office these should go, but the solution to finding them is simple. Write on a piece of paper the name of the item that is too big and put that in your normal allotted file or storage place, with a note of where the item actually is.

IT'S EASY TO KNOW WHAT NEEDS TO BE ACTIONED, BUT HOW DO I DECIDE WHAT TO 'STORE' AND WHAT TO 'DUMP'?

This can be a major problem! The source of some people's disorganization is not laziness or procrastination, but simply their hoarding nature. They keep everything 'because it might come in useful'.

For a personality transplant you may need to read a different book, but I can give you a few key questions to ask yourself about specific items if you are a hoarder, or perhaps live with one and want to influence them:

- Did I remember I had the item until I saw it again?
- Have I had cause to use, wear or need it in the last year?
- Would I suffer any negative consequences if I were to get rid of it?
- Do I need to keep it for legal or tax purposes?
- If it is no longer in full working order, is it repairable at a sensible cost?
- Would I actively miss that specific item if I got rid of it?

How many questions did you say 'no' to? If you are consistently answering 'no', dump it! The only two consistent reasons I hear people say to justify keeping certain items are:

- *Sentimental reasons.* You know what? That's fine. If you have a sentimental attachment to certain things, that is a good reason to keep them. But if you decide to do so, at least organize them and either put the items where you can see them and enjoy your decision to keep them, or store them in a particular storage place. My wife and I have what we call a 'nostalgia bag', a beaten-up suitcase in which we keep all that old rubbish that brings back memories of certain events. It has no intrinsic value or meaning to anyone else. The bag lives in the loft and only comes out very occasionally! If you haven't got one, create one and add to it as you go.
- *Value.* I know people who won't get rid of an item because they say it was expensive when they bought it several years ago, or it may have some commercial value now. I have a couple of responses to this. If it is of commercial value, consider selling it. It is certainly of no benefit in a box in the garage. If you don't want to sell it because of sentimental reasons, then deal with it as above. If it is seriously valuable and you are keeping it as an investment, then it shouldn't be in the pile you're sorting through, it should either be in a bank or a safe or accessible to be viewed or enjoyed!

IF I COME ACROSS ITEMS THAT NEED TO BE ACTIONED AND DEALT WITH, DO I DEAL WITH THEM THEN OR LATER?

This is simple: if it is something serious that has been missed and it is possible to do it within your planned time frame, do it. Regard it as an organizational success that it turned up and you were able to get it sorted. If you are not going to do it then, write into your diary or planner precisely when you will do it. You can then relax, knowing it will turn up at the right time to be dealt with.

TIME MASTER ORGANIZATIONAL TIPS

MAKE SURE THE TIME SPENT ORGANIZING IS PROPORTIONATE TO THE BENEFIT

I know someone who was quite prepared to spend half a day going through three black bin bags of stuff that had been sitting in her garage, loft and store for over five years. Although it needed to be done, the time taken was simply disproportionate to the benefit.

Had there been real things of substance in the bags they would have been missed over the five-year period. As it turned out, the three-hour 'bin bag sort' did turn up a number of precious treasures worth keeping: a yellow plastic boat-shaped pencil sharpener, a knitting pattern and an unused roll of tape!

When sorting your stuff you have to ask: How much time is it worth spending on this task? What is the time–benefit return?

ONLY TAKE TELEPHONE NUMBERS DOWN ONCE

Do you ever scribble somebody's phone number down on a scrap of paper or put a ring around someone's name in *Yellow Pages*? Make a point of either taking the number down in your personal phone number book or onto your contacts list on your computer. This saves you time in hunting for a number over and over.

GIVE EVERY PIECE OF PAPER THE 'ONCE ONLY SAD' TREATMENT

How many times do you handle a document before it finally gets dealt with? I know people who stack their unopened daily post in a pile to process later. They add a few newspapers, some scribbled personal notes, a repeat prescription, a book of stamps and the receipt for a new jumper that needs to be returned for a refund – and they have an organizational disaster waiting to happen. Sound familiar?

There are only three possible actions for each piece of paper that enters your life:

- S = Store it!
- A = Action it – that may include putting it somewhere, having planned precisely when it will be dealt with.
- D = Dump it!

Try to limit the number of times you handle each item. Make your choice as soon as something arrives!

HAVE A GENERAL NOTES SECTION ON YOUR COMPUTER

Use this as you would a scribble pad or the back of an envelope. Put things onto it at random. At the very least you will have things in one place and you can do a computer search to help you find something. I find this particularly useful as I travel a lot and often stay in hotels. I always put the hotel details and booking references into my computer 'general notes' area. It means that I can search for hotels in this section in the future.

CREATE A REMINDER SYSTEM

Disorganized people frequently forget to do things and lose time sorting out the consequences of forgetting.

For example, how do you remind yourself:

- To call the person you promised to phone?
- To send the information you promised by a specific date?
- To transfer money into a particular bank account?
- To pay back someone you borrowed a couple of pounds from?
- To take your medication?
- To post a particular letter?
- To prepare a report you have to present?

The truth is that almost any system will do, provided that it works for you. Time Masters know that there are three important stages to this, so you need to get all of them right. They are:

- Immediacy.
- Visibility.
- Write it down.

Immediacy

The *moment* you know that you will need to be reminded of something, you have to take steps to put your own strategy in place. So if you are on the phone and you promise to call someone at a specific time, put that on your calendar or diary planner *then*. If you borrow some cash from someone, make a note there and then of when you will give it back.

Visibility

Whatever you are trying to remember must have a powerful degree of visibility. Let me give you a few examples of potential ways of achieving this. Choose one of them, or create something that works for you.

- Add the reminder to your mobile phone alarm so that it makes a noise and shows you what needs to be done.
- Put things by the door so that you can't miss them when you leave.
- Write things on a whiteboard or flip chart in your study or office.
- Add what you need to do to your computer reminder system.
- Get someone else to remind you. Have them set a system up as well.

Write it down

Much of the stress of remembering things comes from having to hold them in your head. The solution is simple: write down what you need to do and what you want to remember. This, of course, is where your planning and organizational systems overlap. Write into your diary or planning system when certain things need to be done. Once they are in there, you should be able to relax in the knowledge that they will turn up to be done when the time is right.

IMPROVE YOUR HANDWRITING

If you keep some of your notes in handwritten form, take an extra few seconds to make them legible! I am often so excited about an idea or something I want to get down, I scribble it so quickly that my handwriting leaves much to be desired. I confess there have been times that I have simply been unable to read my own writing.

PUT BACK WHAT YOU TAKE OUT

Another old organizational tip, but still a valuable one: if you get something off a shelf, out of a file or out of a cupboard, then simply put it back as soon as you have used it. Do this even if you think you might need it again soon.

START WITH AND KEEP YOUR DESK OR WORK SPACE CLEAR

Whatever your project, you need to start it with a clear area to do the job. It makes you more efficient, limits the likelihood of you losing things and generally makes you feel better.

My aim, if I am working on a particular book for example, is only to have things on my desk related to that project. If you are cooking in the kitchen, clear away other things so that you can focus on that specific dish or meal.

FOCUS ON THE JOB IN HAND FIRST

Let me explain a typical organizational dilemma by giving you an example.

You are in the process of clearing the clutter from a particular room and sorting it all out. You have set time aside and you are now in the middle of the process. As you are doing it, the curtain rail comes away from the wall and needs to be fixed. Unless you decide to delegate and get someone else to fix it, you will have to identify the problem, decide what you need in order to mend it, go to the shop to buy what you require, get your tools out and do the job.

If you do this, however, it will take up the time you have set aside for clearing the clutter. What do you do? The answer is simple: stick to your plan. Don't get sidetracked. Carry on with your sorting task, but plan when you will do the other fixing job.

The basic rule is don't let a secondary task stop you from carrying out the primary one.

ORGANIZE WHAT IS ON YOUR COMPUTER

Many people think that having files and material stored on a computer means that it is organized. How much time do you spend searching for documents that you know are on your computer, but you just can't remember where you filed them?

With this in mind, build time into your organizational plan to clean up your computer 'stuff'. In practice this means organizing your emails, putting files into meaningful project folders and deleting all the items you don't need any more.

BACK-UP

Back-ups are hugely important. Anything that you value on your computer system needs to be backed up. Time Masters do not want to spend time creating, gathering and storing information only to have to repeat that task again. Anyone who has ever lost documents because of a computer accident, technical problem or theft will know how 'time expensive' this is. Plan your back-ups into your diary and set a loud alarm to go off to remind you.

Let me ask you a simple question. There are three birds sitting on a fence. Two decide to fly away. How many are left?

Three! *Deciding* to fly away is not the same as *actually* flying away!

Deciding to back up your material is not enough: you actually have to *do* it.

4

MASTER YOUR PROCRASTINATION

Are you going to read this section now, or are you going to put it off until tomorrow or next week?!

I have invested a significant amount of my time into researching, speaking and reading about issues related to time management and control. With all this in mind, I have a very cynical question to pose: why do so-called experts want to make everything so complicated and scientific?

On the subject of procrastination, I have encountered tens of thousands of words written by eminent psychologists and thinkers. I could impress you with my grasp of this topic by highlighting the psychological reasons for procrastination; discussing the effects it might have on socio-economic issues;

and even giving you a number of academic definitions and explaining that the word itself comes from the latin *procrastinatus*, meaning to put forward until tomorrow!

The problem with all this, apart from the time it would take for me to write and you to read it, is that you may end up being a bit smarter and better educated, *but* it still won't help you get things done.

If you are a procrastinator – and 20% of people are chronic sufferers – then you put off paying your bills, even if you have the money, miss out on opportunities to buy things when you can get a great deal, pack for holidays at the last minute, shop for presents on Christmas Eve and have a pile of 'things to do' everywhere in your house. Does this sound familiar?

Let's not waste time analysing your feelings over these issues, let's just cut to the process of mastering your procrastination habit.

There are two major reasons for putting things off: the job or task seems to be too big and overwhelming to handle, or it is something you simply don't like doing.

Whichever of these two reasons applies, and sometimes it is both, for most people procrastination is an attitude issue. The cause of your procrastination lies in your thoughts. So to deal with the problem it is your mind and your thoughts that you need to mess with, using some very simple strategies. The most important thing you can do is to understand the constant battle going on in your mind. This is the 'gain' vs the 'pain' match!

Think of it like this. If a job seems to be too big or involves tasks you don't enjoy, then even if you know on a rational basis whatever it is 'needs' to get done, the level of pain often outweighs the gain. And guess what? It won't get done. You'll find or create any number of excuses to justify why you haven't got on with things.

However, if you can reverse the process, by being equally creative in making the task either easier or more pleasurable so that you derive some real enjoyment or gain, then the positive thoughts stand a better chance of winning the match and you are more likely to do what needs doing.

Not convinced? There used to be a television show where a celebrity turned up at someone's home and picked on one member of the family to master some skill or task that they hadn't been great at before. They were given a week to achieve a particular challenge and every member of the family was promised a bumper crop of prizes, such as holidays, electrical goods, clothes and money, if that member of the family was successful in mastering their task.

Guess what? On most occasions the prizes were won. Why? The answer is simple: typically they found a system and method of performing their task that worked for them. They were driven by their motivation to win the prizes and not let their family down.

The same applies to dealing with procrastination. So here are a few thoughts for you to make things easier and create motivation.

TIME MASTER TIPS FOR AVOIDING PROCRASTINATION

BREAK THE TASK INTO BITS

It is often the scale of the task that is the mental obstacle. Sometimes the thought of a particular job or project is so overwhelming that getting started seems impossible. The starting point is not to see the whole job, but to ask yourself the question: 'How can I break this down into very small parts?' Once that is done, all you need to do is to focus on each small part as a whole. Each part in turn becomes the task in hand, rather than the whole job.

CREATE A TIMESCALE WITH A DEADLINE

Once you have gone through the mental process of splitting up a job into manageable, bite-sized pieces, write down when each part can be done based on other time planning you are doing. If in the past you have underestimated how long things take, be smart enough to allow for this in your plan. The act of writing down a timescale for when each bit will get done creates a mental target to aim at. The realization that you *will* get it done and that the task is possible will also give you a real sense of relief.

MAKE IT PUBLIC

No, I don't mean that you have to arrange for national news coverage of your planned tasks. What I do recommend, however, is that you share your plan and intentions with someone else. Once a friend, work colleague or member of your family knows, you have increased the leverage on yourself. There is a degree of peer pressure, which is not a bad thing.

MAKE A GAME OUT OF IT

To the time management purists, what I am about to suggest may seem childish and out of place, but I don't mind because it works. Think about how you can make a bit of fun out of the tasks you don't like doing! Here is a rather personal admission to get the ball rolling: there have been times doing the washing up when I have timed myself, just so I can see whether I can beat my record the next time around. By the way, 3 minutes, 43 seconds isn't too bad. Anyone beat that?

Perhaps a particular piece of music will get you 'up', inspired and through your task? Family members know that the music from *Rocky* works for me!

Seriously, what game can you create out of unpleasant and mundane tasks?

CREATE REWARDS ALONG THE WAY AND AT THE END

Just like the television challenge programme mentioned earlier, what reward can you offer yourself at each stage and at the very end of a task to keep the gain and motivation high?

You might promise yourself that when you have done a particular bit you will take a break, go for a walk and treat yourself to your favourite ice cream with a slab of chocolate in it. The thought of this keeps you going and drives you on.

I'm off for my ice cream at the end of this section of the book and yesterday I booked a week's holiday beginning the day after I'm due to submit the manuscript to my publisher. It would hardly be appropriate for me to be late completing a book called *How to Be a Time Master*!

OTHER FOOD FOR THOUGHT ABOUT PROCRASTINATION

BE HONEST WITH YOURSELF

Some people consistently leave things to the last minute and then complain and blame one unexpected and totally unrelated incident for the delay. For example, you have known you are going on holiday for months. You are now a week away from departure and you still have various personal, domestic and work-related things to get out of the way, but yet you put off doing any of them. Two days before you are due to go, your car breaks down and you *have* to invest some time in getting it sorted. Now you blame your whole last-minute rush on your car: 'If it hadn't been for the car breaking down, I'd have been ready!' Does this sound familiar? Be open and honest with yourself.

PROCRASTINATION IS NOT ALWAYS NEGATIVE

People tend to regard procrastination as a personal weakness. I want to put a slightly different spin on it and encourage you for a moment to recognize that sometimes, 'doing it now' is not always best. Sometimes 'putting things off' might be the right and sensible thing to do.

For example, you might genuinely not be in the right mental or physical state to carry out a particular task. There may well be situations where you need more information before you can make an important decision, or waiting might get you a better deal or, even better still, if you put off the task you can get someone else to do it for you.

In other words, don't confuse procrastination with prioritization. It's okay to put something off because you've redefined your priorities.

BEING SIDETRACKED IS ALSO PROCRASTINATION

I have often seen and heard people fail to get on with a job because they *allow* themselves to become sidetracked. For example, have you ever finally got around to clearing your desk or a pile of papers that has been sitting around for ever, only to find a special offer on something you have contemplated buying? What do you do? You spend the next half hour checking out the deal! Perhaps you decide to watch the television while you hit the ironing pile for half an hour and you end up watching a film for two hours. However good the deal or the film was, you have still spent more time than you wanted doing something you hadn't even considered.

Getting sidetracked is a major problem for procrastinators, as it gives them a pleasurable lever to procrastinate a bit longer.

This is not the Time Master way. It is not controlling your time.

If you are easily sidetracked, you need to identify what it is that pulls you away from your tasks most often and what are your major temptations. Then you need to decide how you can move them out of the way while you get on with what you need to do. In other words, plan and anticipate for the fact that you know you have a habit of getting sidetracked.

Consider physically removing your tempting things from the room where you will be working. If possible turn things off, or even simply avoid a job until a planned or more sensible moment, when it might be acceptable to build in time to indulge yourself.

For example, if you are addicted to Internet games, don't decide at 11.45 p.m., just as you are on your way to bed, to check your emails. The temptation to play for 'just a few minutes' might be too great. Have a planned time the next day to check your emails, or have a specific time slot to play your games, but don't confuse the two!

5

MASTER YOUR TIME ESTIMATES

When I ask people to share with me their personal time problems and weaknesses, high on the league table is underestimating how long things will take. Most people would regard themselves as honest and truthful, yet the vast majority of folk are either hopeless at estimating time or pathological liars! You can decide which category you fall into.

For example, have you ever said:

- I'll be down in a couple of minutes.
- I just need to have a quick shower, it'll only take me five minutes.
- Let's leave that until tomorrow morning, it's only the last few things we need to sort out. It won't take more than 20 minutes.
- We can go through the details of the presentation on the way there. A few minutes should be enough.

The bottom line is this: most of us don't lie deliberately, but we do fail to *think* properly about how long things will take and therefore often convey the wrong impression to others or, indeed, simply kid ourselves. Call me gullible, but if someone says they will take half an hour to do a job, on the whole I tend to believe them.

Someone I know very well has a reputation for being late for almost everything; when she is on time, it has usually involved a mad and stressful rush at the last moment. She tells me, however, 'It is not a question of my punctuality, but that I always underestimate how long things will take.'

This is nonsense. It isn't people underestimating time that causes the problem, the real truth is that people *don't* estimate at all. Estimating time is absolutely critical to mastering your time, to getting control and to becoming a Time Master.

The astonishing thing about this topic is that it is not mentioned in most of the leading time management books. With this in mind, here are a few very simple tips.

TIME MASTER TIPS FOR MASTERING TIME ESTIMATES

BREAK IT INTO BITS

Before giving someone a time estimate for anything, actively and consciously stop and consider what the components of the task are and ask yourself honestly how long each will take. The big problem is that most people look at a collection of simple jobs, roll them together into one and hang a random time frame onto that. For example, having a shower is regarded as a single and simple task. However, if you stop and think about it, it involves several tasks: running the shower; getting undressed; washing, soaping and shampooing in the shower; getting dried; brushing and drying your hair; choosing your clothes and getting dressed. Estimating the time for each job is more likely to give you a better estimate of the total when you think it through like this.

Similarly, in business, a person writing a proposal might initially think it will take a certain amount of time. However, if they break down the tasks into reading the brief; talking it through with colleagues; looking at past projects; costing out any time or items required; typing it up; checking it through; making it look good and sending it off, it is easy to see how it is going to take longer than you might have first thought.

THINK TWICE

Before you tell someone how long something will take, think twice about it. Once you have stated a particular time, they will believe you.

IT IS BETTER AND SAFER TO OVERESTIMATE THAN UNDERESTIMATE

It is rare for someone to think too badly of you because you have got a task done sooner than anticipated.

BUILD IN TIME FOR THE UNEXPECTED

However good you get at estimating, there will be times when unexpected issues and difficulties crop up and conspire to make the job take longer. You might not be able to predict exactly what, but you can allow time 'just in case'.

TIME HOW LONG THINGS TAKE

You don't need to become paranoid over this, but if you know that underestimating is a problem for you, this is a simple strategy that is worth considering. All you need to do is to time how long your most common tasks actually take and compare the reality to your previous expectations. For example, how long does it take you to:

- Draft an average email.
- Read through a standard business proposal.
- Process an order form from a customer.
- Deal with an average sales enquiry.
- Sit down with a cup of tea to read the paper.
- Have a bath.

Once you know how long, you will have two useful tools: first, you can make more accurate estimates in the future and secondly, you will know by what percentage you have been out in the past. You can then allow for this percentage in your future thinking. So if you discover that you regularly take 30% longer to complete a task than your previous estimates, next time around you can add on 30%. Ultimately, this will help you get better control over your time.

6

MASTER YOUR TELEPHONE

If you want to be a Time Master, then you must learn to control the telephone and not let it control you. It is curious that many people don't connect their own lack of time to how much time they allow to be wasted by the phone.

The purpose of this chapter is to highlight some common problems caused by both outgoing and incoming calls and to give you some simple tips to master the phone.

ARE YOU A SLAVE TO THE TELEPHONE?

If you are chatting with your spouse or partner about your day and the phone rings, what do you do? Can you ignore it? Most people simply answer the phone and talk to the caller. Is this you? Are you a phone slave?

There are two problems with this. First, you are sending a message to the person you are chatting with face to face that the telephone and the unknown caller are more important than they are. Definitely not a good strategy with your partner, spouse, client or customer! Secondly, you are not controlling your own time. Your time is being grabbed by whoever has decided to call you at that moment and you are reacting to them.

It is important to understand and remember that the telephone is not to blame, you are. You are the one who chooses to allow your focus and attention to be taken by it. The answer is very simple, but it takes discipline and willpower. Set your voicemail or answerphone!

However, before you do this, ask yourself a simple question: Is the thing that I am doing, or the conversation that I am having, important enough that I want to make it a priority over a ringing phone? If the answer is 'yes', don't hesitate to set your answering and screening facility. Only you can make that decision.

In the office you may be in a sensitive business meeting and don't want to take calls, or at home you might just want to eat dinner undisturbed. On the other hand, if you are expecting responses to a sales or marketing campaign, you might take the view that you should treat that as a high-ranking reason to pick up every call.

DEALING WITH 'TELEPHONE TAG'

How often have you played this game? You call someone who is out, so you leave them a message to call you back. They call you back and this time you are on the phone to someone else.

This can and often does go on for hours and days, leading to a huge waste of time and energy.

You will never avoid telephone tag altogether, but here are some simple tips to minimize the problem.

ARRANGE A SPECIFIC TIME TO SPEAK TO SOMEONE

Sometimes you will actually be speaking with someone on the phone and you agree to get back to them on a particular issue. To reduce the chances of you playing tag in the future, agree a specific date and time to speak to them. As part of the arrangement, tell them that you are putting the call in the diary for that time. They should do the same. As soon as you come off the phone, put the call in the diary if you haven't already done so. Also set a flag or reminder of some sort about the call for a few minutes beforehand, or longer ahead if you need to prepare for it.

Three other quick tips on this:

- Always leave it that you should call them rather than the other way round. This gives you a greater degree of control.
- Double-check the number that they want you to call on.
- Call them at precisely the time agreed.

FIX A SPECIFIC TIME TO SPEAK VIA SOMEONE'S PA

If you are already playing tag, call the person's PA (if they have one) and explain the problem. Have them fix a specific time for you as above.

LEAVE A VOICEMAIL MESSAGE SAYING WHEN YOU WANT THEM TO CALL YOU BACK

For example, 'John, this is Ian. I need to speak to you about the in-house course I am speaking at next Tuesday at your firm, to help you get the most out of the session. Can you give me a call at 9.15 a.m. on Friday? I have blocked out 15 minutes to chat this through with you. If the time doesn't work for you, please email with two alternative time slots for us to talk.' Cynics might question whether this works, but about 85% of the time it really does. Try it.

IF YOU ARE LEAVING A VOICEMAIL MESSAGE, BE SPECIFIC ABOUT WHAT YOU WANT

I have a pet irritation over one particular aspect of playing telephone tag. It is bad enough getting sucked into this when you have a weighty issue that needs to be discussed. But having to play it for no good reason is really annoying. Let me give you an example so that you can avoid this next time.

I received this voicemail message recently from the PA to a key client of mine: 'Hi Ian, could you call me back please? I need to get an important piece of information from you.' I called back and she was out or on the phone. I left a message that I had called. Guess what? She called later on, got my voicemail again and left the same message: 'Sorry, we keep missing each other, could you call me back please? I need to get an important piece of information from you.'

Eventually, after several more calls and a few more notches up the scale on my blood pressure, we finally spoke. What was the important piece of information she wanted? My postal address! Had she been specific in her initial or even her second message – such as saying 'Hi Ian, would you mind letting me have your full postal address please?' – I could have emailed it to her straight away or left her my address on voicemail. Either way, this would have saved both of us spending a disproportionate amount of time on it.

Failure to leave a proper voicemail message can cost the listener time:

- Looking for a number to call back.
- Returning a call to a large organization without a name.
- Worrying about the purpose of the call.

As obvious as it seems, to save yourself and the listener time, good recorded messages should contain four very brief things:

- Your name.
- Your number. Don't gabble it off too quickly. Remember that the person you are calling will probably want to write it down without listening to the message several times. Repeat the number before the end of the message.
- The day and time you are calling.
- A very brief message about the purpose of the call.

HOLD

This is a very simple and obvious solution that you have to make a judgement about, depending on who the person is and why you want to speak to them. If the issue is really important to you and you are told by a PA, for example, that the person is in but on the phone, sometimes it is worth saying, 'I'll hold.' This way you have some certainty and control over what happens.

DO YOU TALK FOR TOO LONG?

I have dealings with people who are virtually monosyllabic on the telephone. Conversely, some people will go on for ever unless stopped. This is true for both business and personal calls.

From a business perspective, it is okay to have a few moments of banter and small talk at the outset of the call as an icebreaker, but most people appreciate you cutting to the chase.

I recently had to review and listen to some recorded sales calls made by someone I was asked to advise. What I heard in some calls was some opening small talk lasting up to 10 minutes and answers to questions also lasting 10 minutes, when 'yes' or 'no' would have been an appropriate response to a simple question.

If you have a tendency to chat over the phone, consider how much time you are giving up.

If you clock up just 15 minutes' unnecessary chitchat each day, that's 75 minutes a week, which equates to almost 2.5 days a year of small talk!

You need to find a balance between being friendly and being too blunt and to-the-point. Sometimes it can be more productive and time efficient to say 'blah' instead of 'blah, blah, blah'!

How much time would you save if you could reduce your telephone talk by just 10% a year?

BEAT THE CALL CENTRE HOLDING CON

Is there anyone who hasn't had the frustration of punching in numbers when trying to get through to a huge organization, only to have to listen to long recorded messages telling you how important you are to them? Yes, we all really believe that! So what can you do to regain control? Here are a few tried-and-tested tips.

CALL THEM AT QUIET HOURS INSTEAD OF PEAK TIME

It's often quicker to phone a call centre first thing in the morning or last thing at night.

KNOW THE SPECIAL 'CHEAT' NUMBERS

Most organizations have a combination of numbers that if pressed will automatically bypass the 'on hold' routine and put you through to a real person.

All you need to do is a simple web search under 'beat call centre queues' and you will be offered many sites with the up-to-date information you need. Many of them give a pretty comprehensive list of major organizations and the special numbers or codes to get you straight through. Do let me know how you get on with this.

BEWARE OF THE PREFIX 0870

Don't dial a number prefixed with 0870. This will often pull you into the organization's queuing system. Call a company's main landline number instead. Try visiting www.saynoto0870.com, a site you can search that will give you the main landline number for many organizations and help you avoid their time-thieving, money-grabbing, poor service tricks.

ARE YOU A MOBILE PHONE JUNKIE?

How much time each day do you spend doing something on your mobile, iPhone or BlackBerry? How did we ever survive for so many years without one? How is it that so many people who claim to be busy can find so much time to chat, text or watch movies on their mobile phone?

Thousands of people seem to be addicted to their mobiles! They walk across busy streets dodging the traffic and chatting on their phone. Despite it being illegal in some countries, how often do you see people talking on their phones while driving? I once saw a coach driver chatting on his mobile held in one hand and peeling an orange with a knife held in his other hand! It rather begged the question of how he was actually steering the bus. Have you ever been talking face to face with someone at a social event, only to find that they keep whipping out their mobile in case a life-changing text has popped up?

If you are controlled and mastered by your mobile, then as bizarre as it sounds, you need to consider the following:

- Turning it off more and more over a set time period in order to cut back gradually.
- Only use it for specific functions or people.
- Reducing the number of people you give your mobile number out to.
- Actually working out how much of your time is going on your mobile.

Many people have mobile phone contracts with at least 600 minutes a month of usage included in the price. If they use that up, as many do, it equates to 7200 minutes in the year, or 120 hours, which translates into a whopping five days a year on the mobile.

You might want to ask yourself if you really want to spend this amount of your life on your mobile phone. Hopefully these figures might make you think twice and cut back.

TIME MASTER TELEPHONE TIPS

- Keep your regular numbers programmed into your phone so that you don't have to keep looking them up and dialling them.

- Plan what you are going to say before calling people. In this way you can minimize the number of times you need to call again because you forgot to ask something.
- Make notes as you are speaking. Talking hands free is very helpful for this, provided that the device is of sufficient quality to give you good sound. Keep your notes in one easy-to-find place afterwards; avoid using random scraps of paper.
- Consider scheduling your outgoing calls for a single block of time if possible.
- Every now and then you will almost certainly be on the end of cold sales calls, which can be intrusive and time consuming. While some people may take malicious pleasure in being rude to callers, this is not my style or the Time Master way. Cold callers have a difficult job and are simply trying to make a living. So I am always polite. As soon as you realize it is a sales call about something you are not remotely interested in, interrupt the caller and say, 'Thanks for the call, but I am really not interested.' If they persist, again interrupt and say, 'I am going to hang up now so you can hopefully do better on your next call.'
- If you do get stuck on hold for a while to someone or indeed to a call centre, switch on the hands-free facility and do something else.

7

MASTER YOUR EMAIL

Handling your email like a Time Master means doing as much as you can to get control over the time you spend in personal email mode. Many people quite reasonably complain about email and information overload, but do absolutely nothing to limit the amount of time they waste handling the never-ending torrent of emails, 75% of which are unwanted promotional junk. I have encountered many folk who have simply given up and accepted 'email time loss' as a necessary evil. The good news is that you don't have to.

Let me be blunt. You can't make the problem go away completely, but you can and should adopt a number of simple damage-limitation strategies to minimize the effect. What you need to do is to ask:

What are the things relating to email overload that I can control?
The answer is that there are several areas of activity that are partially within your personal sphere of influence:

- Control *how often* and *when* you check your emails.
- Control *who* is sending you emails.
- Control *when* you send an email as opposed to other ways of communicating.
- Control *how* you write the email to minimize the problem for the recipient. Often this will be reciprocated.
- Control how you *process* emails to be most time efficient.
- Control the *IT tools* you use to manage the process better.

CONTROL HOW OFTEN AND WHEN YOU CHECK YOUR EMAILS

How often do you check your email? Be honest. I have come across research that indicates it is not uncommon for people to be checking their emails every 5–7 minutes. Here's the sad truth: *frequent email checking is an addiction.* For many it is irresistible and it has got worse as more and more mobile phones and other pocket devices deliver you emails everywhere. Hear the 'ping' and you are lightning quick on the draw as out pops the mobile. You just can't help yourself.

How often have you been chatting or dining with someone and every few minutes the conversation is interrupted by one or other of you hitting your phone for emails or text messages, which are just as bad in this context?

Here is what you need to do.

TURN IT OFF

Yes, turn your email off! I am quite sure there will be times you will turn your answerphone or voicemail on in order to screen phone calls if you are out, away or busy. Do the same with your email. That way you won't be tempted to check when you hear the email 'ping.'

HAVE SET TIMES TO DEAL WITH EMAILS

It is very important as part of the planning process that you decide how often and when you will check emails. For most people more than two or three sessions in the day is not necessary. Once you have done this, forget about your emails until the next scheduled time. This way you control your emails and not the other way around. The object of this is to help you stay focused and to stop you 'just checking'. Almost certainly, if you do keep visiting your inbox you will find things to pull your focus away from other higher-priority things.

I'd like to make a couple of other tips and observations on this issue. If you have enough self-discipline, avoid checking emails for the first half-hour of the day. Doing so asserts your internal mental control at a vital part of the day and stops you getting sucked into whatever has come in overnight. Stick to your 'to do' list priorities.

Many of us survived and prospered before the email revolution. I have very rarely come across an email that was so vital and urgent that it wouldn't keep for 24 hours or more.

CONTROL WHO IS SENDING YOU EMAILS

I accept that none of these tips is absolutely foolproof, but if you become more disciplined you can reduce the volume of emails. Here are a few tips to minimize the number of people who are sending you emails.

GET OFF THE LISTS

If you are regularly getting promotional emails and newsletters from organizations you don't want to hear from, simply 'unsubscribe' from their lists. What many people do is mutter about the emails to themselves and just press delete. That certainly won't stop them coming in the future.

OPT OUT OF ANY DATABASE SHARING

When making purchases of all types of goods or services, you are often asked if the providers can pass or sell on your details or can send you more of their information. Unless you really want them to, *always* opt out.

DON'T GIVE OUT YOUR EMAIL ADDRESS RECKLESSLY

Many people give out their email address to anyone who asks for it. The same applies to people carrying out surveys in the street or shopping centres. Just politely say 'no'.

CONTROL WHEN YOU SEND AN EMAIL AS OPPOSED TO OTHER WAYS OF COMMUNICATING

We all managed to communicate with each other before email was invented. Sometimes you don't have to respond by email just because that is how someone communicated with you. You can and indeed should sometimes pick up the phone and speak to them.

A great example where this might be more efficient is when you're making arrangements to meet up. I have personal experience of an exchange of over eight emails simply to fix the date, time and venue of a business meeting. To shortcut the process I have sometimes spoken to the relevant person on the phone and sorted it all out in one very crisp call.

CONTROL HOW YOU WRITE EMAILS

STOP SAYING 'THANKS'

I wonder how many emails are actually necessary? I have seen many people thank the sender for an email, only to receive a 'thanks' for your 'thanks' in return. Know when to stop! Politeness is good, but one 'thanks' is quite enough.

KEEP EMAILS SHORT

Many email exchanges work very well indeed when kept to a bare minimum. Time Masters know when to be brief in their email correspondence and when it is appropriate to go into more detail.

Someone I have dealt with very successfully for several years never sends me an email longer than a couple of lines. In the context of our exchanges, it is absolutely fine.

CHECK YOUR EMAIL BEFORE YOU SEND IT

Have you ever promised an attachment in your email but forgotten to attach it? What happens? Back comes a reply telling you 'no attachment' and you have to spend time resending. Take a second to double-check that your email is right first time around.

EDUCATE OTHERS IN HOW YOU DEAL WITH YOUR EMAILS

If you instantly respond to emails, that is what others will come to expect of you. If you draft long-winded, chatty and detailed emails, don't be surprised if that is what you get back.

With people you work with a lot or are likely to have dealings with in the future, I strongly suggest that you explain your preferred approach and style and invite them to share theirs. Do this in a friendly way – by email is fine – highlighting that it is in your mutual interests in light of the email overload problem.

CONTROL HOW YOU PROCESS EMAILS TO BE MOST TIME EFFICIENT

ONLY READ THE EMAIL ONCE

When you read your emails during one of your planned sessions, do one of four things with each:

- Reply there and then with a proper response if that is what is needed.
- Ditch it altogether if it is junk mail, and 'unsubscribe' immediately.
- Send a holding or bridging email.
- Plan into your diary or planner when you will deal with it or flag it up in some way.

I suggest you review your emails, skimming through them very quickly to see who they are from, and then decide which is most important to reply to. It's back to prioritizing again. Deal with the most pressing and significant emails first. If something unexpected happens at least those are dealt with and out of the way.

A common mistake is to read all your emails in detail before actually doing anything with them. Sometimes it can be several hours between a first reading and revisiting them. By this time new emails will have been added and you will have to read the original batch again before you can decide how to reply. Hardly a great use of time. Control your emails and you control your time.

REPLY REASONABLY SOON OR SEND A BRIDGING EMAIL

Guess what will happen if you don't reply to a personal, non-junk email within a reasonable period, around three days? The person will email again and now you have twice the stuff on your system. If you can't deal with the email properly after you have first read it, send a polite bridging or holding email to let the sender know when they can expect to hear from you.

CONTROL THE IT TOOLS YOU USE TO MANAGE THE PROCESS BETTER

Managing and organizing your email items and attachments to keep the system streamlined and uncluttered can be, in the long run, a wise time management move. It is no different in importance and concept to organizing your other physical stuff. See the relevant section, 'Master Your Stuff' (page 60). Here are a few simple tips that might help.

DELETE EMAILS FROM YOUR INBOX AND SENT BOX

Get into the habit of regularly deleting items that are filling your inbox and sent box and that you do not need to keep.

GET RID OF EMAILS IN YOUR DELETED ITEMS FOLDER

Although you may have deleted messages, they are merely moved into your deleted or trash folder. Some people have huge numbers of emails stored there. It is a bit like putting things in the wastepaper basket under your office desk but not bothering to empty the bin. Eventually, everything just piles up and creates a mess, which has an impact on your time.

SAVE AND STORE PAST EMAILS

If you have incoming or sent emails and possibly attachments that might be important and that you want to keep for future reference, then save them to a disk, external hard drive or memory stick. Make sure that they are easy to sort and find, however.

SORT MATERIAL INTO FOLDERS AND FILES

Just as you would do with physical, hard-copy materials, set up a system where emails are automatically filed into clients and projects, or even colour coded. Most people will have access to systems that can facilitate this.

GET A NEW, PRIVATE EMAIL ADDRESS

In the same way as you might have an unlisted telephone number, consider getting a separate email address that you only give out to certain people. This will minimize the amount of junk you receive and help you process your emails more quickly.

8

MASTER YOUR SCREEN TIME

Television and the Internet are fantastic. They are a great way to keep in touch with what is going on in the world and a wonderful way to switch off from real life, to relax and lose yourself in an endless world of entertainment. The Internet in particular offers a never-ending, ever-growing, round-the-clock source of information and entertainment and computer games are also a hugely popular competitor for your screen time.

For the less mobile, television and the Internet are a lifeline, a way of staying connected, active and involved. However, if you allow them these media are potentially the biggest time thieves of all and the trainee Time Master's worst enemy!

Let me be very clear about this. I am not being a 'grumpy old man' here – I'll save that for elsewhere in the book – but many people complain about not having enough time to do certain things, yet think nothing of watching every episode of every soap or their favourite drama programme. For many, television controls how they live and plan their time. Many decide when they eat, go to bed, get up, come home from work and even speak to their family based on the timing of certain television programmes.

In theory, the growth of digital television and the possibility of easy, instant recording and replays have resolved this problem. However, in my opinion I think that this technology has made things worse not better, by creating greater television temptation. It is a bit like giving a person who eats too much, a lifetime supply of their favourite chocolate!

The same can be said for the Internet. Many people have to have their daily fix of several hours of their favourite Internet pastime. The problem is compounded by the fact that you can now use the Internet to view television programmes as well.

I know that you've heard all this before. You've probably become immune to clichéd warnings about spending too much time in front of a screen. I don't want to be against televisions or computers, preaching that these are the devil's creations and that you need to cut back; I have done more than my fair share of viewing and browsing over the years.

However, if you feel you are drawn to the television or computer too much but want to be a Time Master, someone who is striving to get control over their time, then reviewing your screen habits and looking at ways of cutting back is a great place to start. The real question is: are you the master of your screens or do they control you? Just make sure you finish this section of the book before you turn the television on...

WHY AND HOW DO YOU VIEW?

Do you ever decide to watch the television and *then* ask yourself, 'I wonder what's on?' How often do you say, 'There's nothing on,' and then spend hours viewing the best of a bad bunch? Is there anyone who hasn't at some time stayed up later than they should, having been hooked by 'the most terrible film' and wondered in the morning, 'Why did I watch that?'

If you have answered 'yes' to any of these, there is one main and overriding time-related reason: *you had nothing better to do!*

When you're busy with a project or other social or personal issues, don't you find that you watch less television? When you're on holiday, how often do you switch on your hotel room TV? Do you sit in your room for hours each night watching whatever comes on? I'll bet you don't.

The truth is that television has become an easy way out, an escape, when you haven't planned what you're going to do. People get into the habit of filling their 'dead time' with the television.

The same concept and rationale also apply to the Internet. How often have you gone online and browsed aimlessly, with no real purpose in mind? I bet you don't do this when you're on holiday or focused on some other interest or activity.

So what is the solution? It's too easy for me to say, 'Turn off your television or computer,' – or, as one high-profile business executive says, 'If you want to get more time, get rid of your television.' The real problem is that television and the Internet can be addictive and can only be dealt with and reduced *if* you have a real desire to do so and sufficient leverage associated with a change in habits.

If you are worried about this issue and have ever considered cutting back, see if any of these simple facts and questions tip the balance and influence you to take real action.

Time Master screen time facts and questions
- Did you know that the average adult watches around 3.5 hours of television a day? If this is you, do you realize that you are spending almost 53 days a year in front of the television? What else could you do with 53 days?
- Are you aware that if you do this from the age of 20 until you are 70, you will have spent over 7.5 years of your life watching television? On your deathbed, do you really want to look back and say this is how you spent all those years?
- Did you know that people now spend twice as much time on the Internet as they do watching television?
- Can you believe that 51% of people between the ages of 10 and 35 spend an average of 12.5 hours a week playing computer games? This equates to 650 hours a year, or almost 27 days a year, blasting, shooting, stealing, flying or thinking their way around various gaming programs.
- Want more sex? Research shows that couples who have a television in their bedroom have sex half as often as those who don't. You know what to do!
- How much time do you spend aimlessly channel hopping and looking at the TV guide to discover there is nothing you really want to watch? Are you aware that 10 minutes a day is over an hour a week and collectively more than two days a year?

If every minute flicking through the channels was worth just 10p, this would be like throwing away £3640 every year!

- How many calories do you consume in front of the television or while surfing the web? Have you made the connection that many people simply eat too much junk food while staring at a screen, making them obese and unfit? What if in every screen hour you consumed 200 calories? How much weight would you lose by cutting your screen time down by half? I have seen research that indicates that 41% of those who are overweight or obese by the age of 26 had also watched a significant amount of television.

- Do you say, 'I'm too busy to get regular exercise' yet spend the average 24.5 hours watching television each week and possibly twice as much time on the Internet? Just an hour less screen time each week would give you time for the recommended minimum of three 20-minute sessions of exercise every week. How much extra lifespan might this give you?

- What are you really giving up by spending so much time staring at a screen? What are you leaving undone?

- If you just gave up 10–20% of your screen time, how much more could you achieve?

- Did you know that too much screen time actually makes you feel tired and depressed?

- Did you know that brain scans show that the thinking part of the brain slows or shuts down while watching television?

- Have you considered that watching so much television makes you one of life's spectators rather than a participant? Is that really what you want?

- Got a neck or back problem? Get frequent headaches? Did you know that too much time on the Internet is a contributory factor to these problems?
- Have you ever encountered people who have nothing else to talk about but television programmes, websites or the quality of the graphics on the latest computer game? Do you want to turn into one of them?

Again, let's just put all this into perspective. Television, the Internet and computer games aren't all bad. In fact quite the contrary, their contribution to the modern world is enormous. Like everything else, however, it is a question of moderation. If you want to be a Time Master and to control and master your time, you *must* master your screens.

Each day, children in the UK spend an average of 2.7 hours watching television, 1.5 hours on the Internet and 1.3 hours on a games console. This is 5.5 hours in front of a screen every day – 2007 hours a year! This is more hours than they spend in a classroom or interacting with their parents.

TIME MASTER SCREEN TIPS

- Be selective with the television programmes you watch. Choose and plan what you watch more carefully. Decide what you *really* want to see each week and record those programmes. Then plan precisely *when* you want to view them. This way you are taking control and not reacting to the programme scheduler's whims.

- Use the Internet for specific purposes only and then get off it. Stay focused on that objective and don't get sidetracked by websites or pages that are outside that task. If you see something else that interests you, plan when you will visit it.

- Get busy with something else. Become more actively involved with your outside interests, hobbies and commitments.

- As part of your time planning, actively decide in advance each week how you would like to spend your free time. Would you really write 'Watch television', 'Browse the Internet' or 'Play computer games' into your diary? If so, that's fine, but establish times for doing this. It then becomes a controlled activity.

- Instead of saying to the family, 'What shall we watch?' try asking, 'What game would you like to play?' The answer might well be an interactive computer game, but at least this is involves some social interaction.

- If you are really serious about reducing your viewing hours, consider removing the television or computer from the bedroom. The more convenient they are, the more you will end up looking at a screen.

- The more screens you have in the house, the more screen time will be clocked up. Again, consider reducing the number of screens you possess.

- If you really want to give yourself a shock, log how many hours a day you and members of your family actually spend on the web, watching television or playing computer games. Multiply this to get an annual number of hours and then multiply it again to see how much time you will have given up by the age of 70. Use this figure as a lever to force yourself to cut back. Have a competition to see who can reduce their hours the most.

- If you are passing through a room where the television is on, don't pause or stop to see what is showing. Just keep walking to where you were going.
- If you are determined to reduce your screen hours in order to create more time for other things, consider doing this gradually by setting yourself relatively easy targets. For example, cut back by 10% or one hour every week.
- Find the off switch!

9

MASTER YOUR MEETINGS

To be blunt, if you want to find a way of wasting time at work or anywhere else for that matter, have a meeting!

Have you *ever* been to a meeting, particularly an internal company one, where you left feeling uplifted and excited, like you had really achieved something useful and this was a great use of your time?

I have, but not often. I have spent many frustrating hours sitting in various business, corporate, social and charitable meetings and committees that have been an utter waste of time. I struggle to think of more than a few that have been necessary and totally constructive. There seems to be a culture in many organizations of simply holding meetings as a substitute for actually getting on with the job!

- Business people and executives spend between 25% and 80% of their working time in meetings, yet between a third and a half of all meetings are regarded as a waste of time.
- People switch off completely just 41 minutes into a meeting. Over three quarters lose attention after just 15 minutes.
- 9 out of 10 people daydream in meetings.
- 60% of meeting attendees take notes to appear as if they are listening.

The reality, of course, is that meetings are more often about internal politics, the management of internal decision-making and 'back covering' than anything else.

It never ceases to amaze me how much time is squandered in meetings. I once attended a formal gathering of a major legal practice at which 20 partners were present, all of whom charged about £250 an hour. The only issue to discuss was what percentage shade of grey their new brochure front cover should be printed in. This discussion went on for three hours! If you do a bit of basic number crunching, this vital meeting and decision cost them 60 hours of time; at their charging rate, that's £15000. Time and money well spent, don't you think?

It is astonishing and ironic that one of the things business people spend so much of their work time on is regarded by them as one of the biggest time traps of all. Here are just a few of the comments I have heard when I have asked people about meetings in their organization:

- 'Given email and other modern ways of communicating with each other, it is incredibly outdated to think that every time we need to speak to each other we have to have a meeting.'
- 'We have weekly marketing meetings, monthly departmental meetings and quarterly partners' meetings. Every time we discuss virtually the same things. We talk a lot and no one ever does anything.'
- 'On the whole I think meetings here are a waste of time. The only good thing about them is that I can stock up on sandwiches, fruit and chocolate biscuits.'

Of course, some meetings *are* productive and justified. What is it that differentiates the worthwhile from the time-wasting meetings? Here are some of the issues to consider, with some Time Master tips on how to master your time when it comes to meetings.

MEETING OBJECTIVES

Are there potential tangible benefits to *all* parties of having this meeting? If you can't identify them, don't meet! Some one-to-one sales or relationship meetings are advantageous, for example, as are internal meetings to make a decision and take action on a specific issue, or even to brainstorm ideas.

However, if a meeting is called just for the sake of meeting, or to report on progress on a particular project, there are more time-economic ways of doing this.

ALTERNATIVES TO MEETINGS

Is there a better way to facilitate an exchange of information than a face-to-face meeting? The reality is that there are other options. Email, telephone, conference and web meetings can now replace time-consuming travelling to meetings. At least consider these first.

KEY PEOPLE

A classic mistake is that often key people can't be at a meeting for one reason or another. Despite this, I have still seen many a meeting go ahead simply because it has been scheduled. Let's be clear on this, if the discussion revolves around a specific person being in attendance because of their knowledge, experience or involvement in a particular project and they are not able to be present, then cancel or postpone the meeting.

NUMBERS ATTENDING

I have frequently encountered situations where a whole department or team of people are invited to the meeting so that some of them don't feel 'left out'. This is a political problem, which can be easily solved by good leadership, communication and management. As a basic rule, the more people that are present, the less constructive the meeting will be.

PREPARATION AND HOMEWORK

Meetings are often held without an agenda or a written list of issues to be discussed. It is good practice from a time management point of view to have a list of discussion points. This rule holds good for one-to-one meetings too. 'Just a few things to go through, so I've jotted down an informal agenda,' you might say as you open your notebook. It is a very useful way of taking control both of the meeting and of your time.

STARTING AND STOPPING ON TIME

Meetings should always start punctually and have a formal time to finish. If the meeting ends earlier so much the better, but it should never overrun. Remember the Time Master Truth about thinking in hour and half-hour time frames (page 21)?

MEETING MINUTES

Another meetings convention is the reading of minutes. There are times when this is sensible, indeed even a legal requirement, but the formality of minute taking and reading isn't always necessary or helpful, particularly in informal situations where it just soaks up time. I have attended many meetings that start by reading the minutes followed by discussion of them. Why?

Often the agenda can be structured so that you cover relevant items anyway. People who missed a previous meeting should have read the minutes beforehand if they were circulated, assuming that they wanted to.

TOO MANY CORPORATE OR DEPARTMENTAL COMMITTEES

A simple way to reduce the amount of time drained by meetings is to have fewer different committees. Does your organization really need multiple committees for decision-making?

One client I was advising had a hierarchy of four committees with varying degrees of authority. It took six months of debate and discussion by all committees, each of which consisted of five people, to approve a simple, non-provocative recommendation that cost £60!

DATE OF NEXT MEETING

There is a convention that before one meeting ends, the date for the next meeting should be fixed, and this is often an agenda item. This has become a habit in many organizations and committees. A better question might be, 'Do we need to hold another meeting at all?' Perhaps there are times when you can simply leave things until a matter arises that needs a discussion.

PROTECT AND VALUE YOUR OWN TIME

The number of meetings you hold is not a barometer of success. I know of one managing director who arranges meetings pretty much anywhere in the country simply because someone asks if they can meet. She recently put two hours in the diary for a client meeting. It took two and a half hours to get there and on arrival the client passed her a written brief on a sheet of paper and made small talk for 10 minutes. She then had a two and a half hour journey back!

This is a classic example of a meeting that was arranged with little regard for time. A quick phone call planned for a specific time, together with a fax, letter or email with the briefing document, would have saved several hours. How much time do you lose attending unnecessary external meetings?

BE OPEN ABOUT 'MEETING AVOIDANCE' STRATEGIES

People regularly email or call me asking to meet to discuss 'collaboration'. Usually that means that they want to sell me things or for me to endorse their products. Even if I think, based on my 'gut feel', that it might be of interest, I almost never agree immediately to the meeting they are suggesting. Instead I say, 'In the interests of both your time and mine, let's first of all arrange a specific and convenient time to talk on the phone for five minutes, to establish if there really is any mutual ground.'

MAKE TIME A KEY ISSUE WHEN YOU START A MEETING

Have you ever had a meeting with someone that's started with a bit of small talk and a coffee, only to learn that the person you are seeing, whom you want to ask for something, has to leave in 10 minutes? You then feel under pressure and find it difficult to achieve your objectives. You may also have experienced the same sort of situation the other way around, where the person you are talking to expects more time from you than you want to give.

You can both protect your own time and be respectful of someone else's by asking, 'How much time do you have?' very early on.

If somebody has agreed to meet with me, as a matter of routine I normally ask right at the beginning of the meeting, with a smile on my face:

'Listen, thanks very much for seeing me. So that I don't overstay my welcome, can I just ask how much time you are okay for?'

If it is me who has agreed to see someone, I might ask at the outset:

'Thanks very much for coming in. I don't know how you're fixed, but I'm okay for the next 20 minutes before my next engagement. Is that going to be okay for you?'

You don't even need to wait until the beginning of the meeting itself to raise this issue. I recommend that you build a discussion of time into your initial arrangements so that both parties know beforehand how much time will be taken up. These sorts of questions facilitate efficient and positive use of time and also enhance business results and output.

TAKE PHONE NUMBERS WITH YOU TO MEETINGS

Ever been held up on the way to a meeting and wanted to call to say you were running late, but couldn't because you didn't have the number to hand? Always make sure you have a contact number. Build that into your pre-meeting planning.

THINK CAREFULLY ABOUT REFRESHMENTS

There is a compromise to be reached between being friendly, hospitable and creating an appropriate atmosphere and automatically doing the 'coffee or tea' thing, which will add time. I attended a meeting the other day that was coming to its natural conclusion, when unexpectedly the door opened and, without having been asked, a secretary carried in a tray of coffee and biscuits. In the interests of politeness, we then ended up spending an extra 15 minutes making small talk before we could leave.

I am not saying you should avoid refreshments, but at least be aware that this will add time to a meeting, so factor it in before deciding one way or the other.

DOUBLE-CHECK THE MEETING VENUE

If you have responsibility for setting up meetings, always double-check the room before the meeting itself. I have witnessed on many occasions an incredible amount of time wasted because rooms had been double-booked, weren't set up properly or didn't contain the right facilities.

10

MASTER YOUR INTERRUPTIONS

Interruptions will almost certainly be one of your time issues. Just for the record, you're not the only one. Interruptions rank pretty high on almost everyone's time problem list. With this in mind, whatever you do, don't answer the phone while reading this section!

People tend to get one interruption every eight minutes. With the average interruption taking five minutes, this is about 50% of the work day.

To give you some indication of the scale of this problem, 80% of interruptions are typically rated as of little or of no value, and many people don't even regard them as interruptions.

What is absurd about this problem is that the victim usually blames the person or thing that is allegedly responsible for the interruption. How often have you said through gritted teeth, 'The telephone rang,' or 'Someone just popped in.'

Let me say something provocative that you won't find in any other book on time management or control. In most cases, an interruption only takes place if you allow it to. The truth is that *you* are to blame for virtually all your interruptions.

You choose to answer the phone or allow someone into your office. While you will never get rid of all interruptions, there are many things you can do to minimize them. Here are a few painkilling solutions for you to consider, remembering that the vast majority of interruptions happen through someone turning up in person or via some piece of technology or a physical issue. This includes the telephone, text, email, a pager or a mobile phone.

UNPLANNED VISITORS

PRIORITIZE YOUR INTERRUPTIONS

The first thing you have to do is adjust your mindset and realize that not all interruptions are bad. I have read in some time management materials that the way to deal with unanticipated folk who interrupt us is 'just say no'. You should be wary of this approach. Of course there *will* be times when you need to send the 'have you got a couple of minutes' or 'social chitchat' people packing, but be careful because there will equally be times when you *should* allow yourself to be interrupted.

The first tip, therefore, is to appreciate the need to prioritize your interruptions, recognizing that there are good interruptions as well as bad. If a potential customer you have been trying to generate business from wants to speak to you to give you an order, I don't think it would be unreasonable to break off what you are doing and take the call. What is most important is that you get into the habit of asking yourself the simple Time Master Interruptions question:

Is the potential interruption of greater or lesser value than the task I am currently doing?

By doing this you at least stand a chance of being able to distinguish the good interruptions from the bad. Most people don't ask this question. They either break off what they are doing, thinking dark thoughts about the person who is interrupting, or they take malicious pleasure in telling them to come back later.

There is a lovely cartoon of a medieval battle complete with archers firing their arrows at the enemy and being shot at by the opposing archers. An automatic machine gun salesman is approaching the commander and being turned away with the phrase: 'Can't you see I'm busy?'

Deciding on the relative importance of an interruption isn't an exact science. Sometimes you will get it right and at other times you won't, but that is at least a better strategy than turning away every possible interrupter without question.

So next time someone walks into your office and asks, 'Have you got a couple of minutes?' say politely but firmly, 'Actually, I'm in the middle of something right now, can it wait?' or 'Is it something urgent?' or if it is your boss, 'Do you mind me asking whether it's more important than...' and describe what you're doing at the time. This is a positive strategy that gives the other person the chance to tell you what they want, while getting the message across to them that unless it is of a higher priority than your task, they will have to wait.

If you do decide you are prepared to break off what you are doing, don't just dive in. Explore with the other person some other questions:

- Do we need to discuss this now?
- Okay, I agree we need to talk about this, but let's fix a specific time later.
- Exactly how long will this take? I'm really stretched at the moment.
- Is there anyone else you can talk this through with?

This open but questioning approach is the Time Master way, as it maximizes your control over your time.

You will only have to adopt this strategy once or twice and most people will learn for themselves when to bring you things and when to stay away. It is part of educating others that you regard your time as valuable and that you want to protect and control it.

CLOSE YOUR DOOR

This is an obvious and easy solution, but many people simply don't do it. It is absolutely fine to close your door to show others that you don't want to be disturbed from a particular task. It doesn't mean that people can't interrupt, but it does force them to think twice. This will reduce the number of wasted interruptions.

You could even put a sign on the door: 'Time Master at work…urgent interruptions only!' or some other tongue-in-cheek message.

CONTROL UNPLANNED VISITORS THROUGH YOUR ACTIONS

If you have allowed an unplanned visitor into your office, room or home, you can minimize how long they are with you by your actions and behaviour. If you offer them a seat and a coffee, don't blame them for staying for a while. That's the message you are sending. If you stay standing to chat, or you don't offer them a seat, or you keep piles of papers on your visitor's chair or you start packing your papers away, most folk will get the hint that you have other things to do. All these are easy tips to manage interruptions.

DISCOVER THE GOOD AND BAD INTERRUPTERS

Take note of people who are time wasters and those who bring you acceptable or sensible interruptions. By doing this you can begin to prioritize when you should say 'come in' and when 'not now' with a greater degree of accuracy.

Some time management experts recommend keeping an 'interruptions log'. You track and rate each interruption during the day for a set period of time, in order to see who gives you the most useless or important interruptions. If you think it might be helpful to you, then this is a practical step you can take. My personal experience is that I don't need a time-consuming logging system to tell me the precise statistics of a particular time waster. I expect you already know who yours are too!

PLAN YOUR INTERRUPTIONS

This is another simple strategy that is often missed. If you know from experience that you regularly get people popping in with questions and issues, actually plan into your day when you want this to happen and make sure that everyone knows. If you do get visitors, then you are controlling them and not the other way around. If nobody turns up, you can carry on with your other tasks. How often you build interruption times into your daily plan and for how long is obviously a matter for your discretion based on your position and role.

HAVE INTERRUPTION-WISE GATEKEEPERS

If you are important enough in your organization to have a secretary or PA, you need to give them this section of the book to read, or better still buy them their own copy! They too must be educated in the notion of 'good' and 'bad' interruptions. These people are often known as 'gatekeepers', with the reputation of being inflexible and overzealous about keeping everyone out. If you are a gatekeeper, then almost on a daily basis you should ask your boss, 'When can you be interrupted and under what circumstances?'

CHANGE THE POSITION OF YOUR DESK

Many people tell me that one of the causes of interruptions is the physical layout of their office. If you work in an open-plan environment, turning your desk around so that you are facing in another direction may prevent you from making eye contact with passers by and thus reduce casual, chitchat interruptions from them.

INTERRUPTIONS FROM THE TELEPHONE, EMAIL, TEXT ETC.

It is quite astonishing how simple most of the following tips are and yet so many people overlook them, or are too weak to embrace them.

TURN YOUR MOBILE OFF AND YOUR VOICEMAIL ON

People are always telling me that they can't get things done because the phone keeps ringing. Ask yourself as you start a project or task: 'Is this important enough that for a set time I don't want to be disturbed?'

If the answer is yes, simply turn off your phones so that your answering facility takes the calls. However, record a specific message to say something like, 'I am unable to take your call at the moment, but I am around and will be available to return your call by such and such a time, so please leave a message.'

This is important, because it transparently indicates when you will be available to listen to the message and when you can return the call. This encourages the caller to speak instead of ringing off and people will respond well to your good communication. The normal blunt, 'I'm out' kind of message does nothing to help your callers.

Some folk have said to me that they like to be available all the time for customers and clients. This is a noble sentiment, but a naïve one. Accept now that you can't be and that it is not even in their long-term interests that you should be. In most cases you have to build in some uninterrupted time to process work for customers and clients and do whatever you have to do for them. That is good customer service too.

TURN OFF YOUR EMAIL

The same principle applies to emails. Turn your email off for a set time when you have something important to do that you want to focus on exclusively. This removes the temptation to check your emails, something that many people do every few minutes. (See Chapter 7 for more on dealing with email overload.)

Always remember the Time Master Truth: put yourself and your family first! There should be times when you are doing personal and domestic things, like being on holiday. When you are, switch off your business and work-related emails. If you don't you are never, ever off duty and others control your time.

It is also good practice, if you have the facility, to set an 'out of office' response so that any emailers know you are not around and when you will be back. Deal with your emails at planned sessions during the day.

11

MASTER YOUR TIME THIEVES

A time thief is quite simply a person or an organization that steals your time. In just the same way that you need to be vigilant and street wise against pickpockets and theft from your home, you need to be alert to those companies, red-tape 'jobsworths' and individuals who rob you of your valuable time without a second thought. Time Masters do what they can to keep control and minimize the time cost to themselves, or at the very least seek to express their views to prevent time theft becoming an acceptable offence.

You need to be able to recognize a 'time thief' and know some simple tips to avoid being a victim or minimize the consequences.

COMPANY TIME THEFT

If being a time thief isn't bad enough, some companies actually make you pay for the privilege of stealing your time and then have the temerity to attempt to pass it off as good customer service. For example, various travel companies charge you for calling their customer service helplines and making you queue while you wait for the next available adviser. Still as the message goes, they do value your patience – no wonder at 10p a minute!

Hotels have also perfected the art of stealing your time while getting you to believe it is in the interests of good service. Nowadays the buffet breakfast is common, where you get your own food. This is supposed to put you in control. However, it has now become the norm to stand for several minutes watching your toast cook on a painfully slow rotating machine that you personally feed with bread. Still, it is a great networking opportunity…

If that isn't bad enough, only a few weeks ago I encountered something new: a hotel where I had to cook my own boiled eggs! What next? Will I end up with a shopping list on my pillow at night instead of a chocolate? Joking apart, there is something wrong with service organizations putting prices up, giving less service and stealing our time.

TIME MASTER TIPS FOR HOTELS

ASK FOR HELP

If you ask a member of hotel staff to assist, they usually will. Ask politely: 'I'm really pushed for time this morning, I'd be grateful if you could get me a couple of slices of toast please.' The more you do yourself, the more time will be taken and this will become the norm.

GIVE APPROPRIATE FEEDBACK

Every time you are asked to fill in one of those service comment cards, include your objection to any deliberate system that steals your time and indicate that you will actively seek a different hotel in the future that has a different policy.

SERVE NOTICE

Serve the hotel (or any other company) with a 'Time Master – Guilty of Time Theft Notice' available on the Time Master website www.beatimemaster.com. Simply print it off, fill it in and send or give it to the offending company, individual or manager and then add it to the corporate Time theft section of the website. Hopefully, the double pressure of being given this document and of having it in the public domain will serve as some type of deterrent.

TELEPHONE TIME THEFT

If you have ever telephoned a company and spent minutes listening to a recording telling you what number options to press, only to be greeted with, 'All our agents are busy at the moment,' and then ended up on hold for the next 20 minutes, then you have been the victim of time theft. Some organizations even compound the offence by charging you for being on hold and playing you advertizements at the same time.

Perhaps you call an organization and have to listen to a long list of recorded options. If yours is Option 8, you can have been connected for two minutes before you can even press the relevant button.

Strategies have been explained fully in 'Master Your Telephone' (page 94), but just to recap:

- Call at quiet hours instead of peak time.
- Know the special numbers, a combination of numbers that automatically bypass the 'on hold' routine and put you straight through to a person.
- Beware of the prefix 0870 – call the company's main landline number instead.

RED TAPE TIMEWASTERS

Typically, organizations create rules for their own, sometimes bizarre reasons, and then its employees park their common sense and stick to the letter of those rules. How about this little gem?

After a university lecture, my son decided to go to the departmental office in the same building to see if one of his assignments was marked and ready for collection. It was. However, the person on the desk refused to give it to him, saying, 'We have to email you first, to tell you it's ready for collection.' He had to walk the 20 minutes home, check his emails to find the relevant notice, so that he could then return to collect it. Those three extra walks cost him an hour. At least the exercise was good for him!

TIME MASTER TIPS FOR RED TAPE

- Complain in writing to a senior person in the organization. Don't get embroiled in a time-consuming argument, but at least politely and clearly make your opinion known.
- Offer the organization a constructive alternative that helps them deal with the issue behind their rule.
- Serve the company with a 'Time Master – Guilty of Time Theft Notice' as explained on page 141.
- Write a brief note about the problem to the press, who love stories highlighting bureaucratic bungling and stupidity. If the story is used, it may serve as a lever to get the rule changed; if it doesn't, you may feel better anyway having got your frustration off your chest.

THE WAITING-IN SCENARIO

Ever had to wait in for a delivery or for someone to arrive to do some work for you? 'They'll be with you between 8 a.m. and 6 p.m.,' you're told when things are arranged. Apart from the sheer frustration of this, the organization has potentially robbed you of your time and certainly your control.

TIME LORD TIPS FOR DELIVERIES

- Ask to be the first call of the day. Many organizations will do this if you request it.
- Ask for the driver or someone to call you an hour before they plan to get to you.
- Ask for the mobile numbers of the drivers or staff so that you can call them.

- Ask whether the company can at least narrow it down to morning or afternoon.
- Call the administration number during the day to check on progress.
- Serve the company with a 'Time Master – Guilty of Time Theft Notice' as above if its staff don't turn up as promised.

PERSONAL TIME THIEVES

It is not just companies that are guilty of time theft, individuals do it too.

PEOPLE WHO ARE OFTEN LATE

Ever agreed to meet someone at a given time, only to hang around waiting for them because they are late? Once may be an accident – problems can often crop up – but twice or more and they begin to look like serial time thieves.

Sometimes the people you deal with in business, work or your personal life are a matter of choice. If you discover that certain folk are time thieves and you are a regular victim, think twice whether they are right for you.

DON'T FALL FOR THE 'COUPLE OF MINUTES' LIE

How often have you heard these phrases?

- I'm just popping out for a couple of minutes.
- I'll be back in a couple of minutes.
- I'm on my way, I'll only be a couple of minutes.

The truth is that it is almost never a couple of minutes. If you accept the statement – and sometimes you have little choice – be prepared to wait longer or give up more of your time.

IF PEOPLE ARE KEEPING YOU WAITING, CALL THEM

If someone is running late, always try to call them to find out where they are. This seems like an obvious thing to do, but many people don't do it at all or say, 'I'll just hang on a quarter or half an hour, and then I'll call.' Phone if you can and try to get some certainty. This way you retain control and have a chance of using the waiting time most effectively.

INTERRUPT

Do you know people who just go on and on? They call you on the phone and never stop talking, or you meet them in the street and just can't get away. These people are also time thieves. You have to be assertive and tell them at the outset of the conversation that you can't talk for long, then jump in and say, 'I'm really sorry to interrupt, but you'll have to forgive me, I'm really pressed for time today, so I'll have to go.'

12

MASTER THE ABILITY TO SAY NO!

Have you been asked if you can do something that involves your time? You hear your brain scream, 'Absolutely not!' only to find your lips moving quite independently and saying, 'Of course, no problem, I'd be delighted. Anything else I can do for you as well?'

Many people live in their own world of being overwhelmed and stressed, sometimes quite literally at screaming pitch because they perceive that they don't have enough time to do everything. They spend fortunes on planning and time management techno-gadgetry, but in many cases all they need to do is learn to say 'no'. Part of my role in this book is to tell you that 'no' is okay! You are allowed to say it.

If the ultimate aim of being a Time Master is to get maximum control over *your* time, then if you always say 'yes' you are permanently at risk. You have effectively handed over control to anyone who might ask you to perform a task or a favour for them.

Why is this simple truism so difficult for so many people? I have come across many who say 'yes' far too often and really struggle to say 'no'. Here are a few of the reasons:

- *The person asking is your boss!* This really can be tricky. The added leverage of your respective positions can create additional pressure on you to take on more than you feel you can cope with. However, in the long term you can't say 'yes' to everything. Sooner or later you need to develop ways of saying 'no' that don't compromise your standing with your boss. I will give you a number of suggestions later.
- *Desire to please and guilt.* You may simply feel uncomfortable saying 'no', as if you are letting the other person down. Your natural instincts have been honed over the years to believe that it is good to please and to help others. In many cases this is a personal strength, yet taken to extremes it can also be a huge weakness. If you aren't careful you end up accommodating everyone else but yourself. Part of being a Time Master is realizing that you are important too!
- *Not knowing how.* Believe it or not, some people are quite prepared to say 'no' some of the time, they just don't know how to do it. I give you 20 ways below for you to adapt to your own style, personality and the specific situation.
- *Loss of opportunity.* Sometimes you find it difficult to say 'no' because the request seems like a great opportunity that you

can't pass up. It may be a possible sales or business opportunity, or just a great part you've been offered in your local amateur drama group that will involve weeks of rehearsals and line learning.

In these sorts of situations, the pressure is internal and comes from the thought of what you might be giving up. Accepting that you might need to relinquish certain things is part of the Time Master philosophy. Ultimately it is all about you deciding on your priorities and continually re-evaluating them. Once you have done that, however, based on some of the questions and tips I highlight in the section of the book on 'Master Your Priorities' (see page 54), decide to say 'no' to your lowest priority if you can't find a way to do everything.

In business situations there will be occasions where you are approached because of your personal reputation or a recommendation. I can tell you from long experience of these sorts of situations that 90% of people who contact you on this basis *will* be prepared to wait a reasonable amount of time to get you. Have the courage to make them wait rather than overstretching yourself out of a feeling that you have to instantly accommodate their time frame. I can guarantee you will rarely lose a job simply because you try to arrange it to your timescale.

20 TIME MASTER WAYS OF SAYING 'NO'

- 'I'm sorry, I really have to focus on other priorities for the time being.'

- 'Do you know what, I'm right in the middle of other projects at the moment. It's just not a good time for me right now. I may be able to get to it next week or month. Would that be okay?'
- 'It's kind of you to think of me, I'm really flattered, but I am not taking on any new responsibilities at the moment.'
- 'I'm sorry but the answer has to be 'no'.'
- 'I have just got too much on my plate at the moment and I honestly don't know when I would be able to get to it. If I can suggest someone else would that be helpful?'
- 'Before I take this on for you, let me give you a few tips that might help you do it for yourself.'
- 'I have made so many commitments to others, it would be unfair to let them down by saying 'yes' to you and overstretching myself by taking on too much at this point.'
- 'It's always nice to be asked, but I'm just not the best person to be doing this for you right now.'
- 'Now that's the type of thing I'd have really loved to help you out with, if only I had the time.'
- 'I hope you don't mind me being really honest with you. This is just not for me, I simply don't enjoy doing that. Thanks anyway.'
- 'It's very tempting to say 'yes' but I'm trying to be really strict with myself and manage my time better at the moment. I have had a weakness for saying 'yes' too often in the past. I'm sure you understand.'
- 'I hope you'll forgive me saying 'no', I need to devote my energies to my job and career at the moment.'

- 'I just can't right now, I want to devote more of my time to my personal and family life.'
- 'It would be very easy to say 'yes', but I need to free up more time for myself right now.'
- 'Given how much I have on at the moment, it would be fairer for both of us for me to decline than to say yes and risk doing less than my best work.'
- 'I was close to saying 'yes', but something unexpected has come up that needs my urgent attention.'
- 'I can't right now, but is it okay if I come back to you as soon as I am in a position to help?'
- 'I'd prefer not to go into details, but I think you know me well enough to know that when I say 'no' it's for a good reason.'
- 'I'm sorry but I just can't cope with anything else just now. The good news is that I have someone else who can help.'
- 'I'm afraid I have this report to finish by 2 p.m. today first. Can it wait until then?'

TIME MASTER TIPS FOR SAYING 'NO' TO YOUR BOSS

If having a boss who overloads you with work with no real understanding is your problem, then turn to page 152 as I have a whole chapter entitled 'Master Your Boss'. Here are some other general tips.

DON'T BE A 'JUSTER'

A 'juster' is someone who says, 'I'll *just* do this one more thing,' 'I'll *just* fit in one more meeting,' 'I can *just* get one more proposal written before close of play.' Is this you? The more 'justing' you do, the less control you will have. Have the self-control to say 'no' to yourself as well.

THINKING IT OVER

It is also okay to ask for a bit of time to think through whatever it is you are being asked to do. Just be careful that you don't ask for time simply to delay saying 'no' straight away. If you encourage someone to think there is a possibility you might agree to something, it is harder to back off later on.

SET EXPECTATIONS AND GET PERMISSION

From a work point of view, it might be a good idea to discuss possible time overload issues before they arise, when you first start the job and you are discussing your role. This way it can make this aspect easier to deal with if a problem occurs.

YOU DON'T ALWAYS NEED TO EXPLAIN

Unless what you are being asked to do is part of your job description, you don't need to feel you have to explain why you are saying 'no'.

13

MASTER YOUR BOSS

Most of the focus in time management books is on getting yourself in shape so that you can plan, prioritize and control your own time better. That is what being a Time Master is all about. That is fine, but on a day-to-day, practical basis, the problem that some people have is a shambolic boss.

This is someone who typically makes endless demands on your work and personal time, with no real thought about you. They are often so bad at time management themselves that you end up attending regular, pointless, time-wasting, badly run meetings they have called and sorting out *their* hopeless inefficiency. Sound familiar?

The bottom line is that however good you are at managing and mastering your own time, if you have a boss who is a novice Time Master, this will affect your life and your time control. I'm not talking about the work-related things that many folk choose to do, like taking work home sometimes, which is often an accepted part of their role. For example, teachers may not like the endless marking of students' work and lesson preparation, but on the whole they know that what they can't get done at work needs to be done at home and it is simply part of the job.

The real and more sinister problem, however, is when you feel you have no choice. This is when you are compelled to work after hours or attend weekend meetings in order to keep your head above water, or simply out of political or peer pressure. Often this problem is insidious, in that it starts out with the odd 10 minutes here and there, but eventually turns into the norm.

This short section is also a gentle reminder to all bosses, employers and managers! The likelihood is that you are reading this book to improve your own skills for your own purposes, but if you are responsible for other people and how they spend their time, you also need to help not hinder them. If they work time-productively they are more likely to be more content and efficient, which is to everyone's benefit, including yours.

The workplace is full of stressed people trying to cope with what they perceive as too much to do in too little time. It is a fact that in many cases employers and managers heap more work, projects and responsibility on people who are already sinking fast. What do these people do? Conscientious and sensitive people start coming in earlier, staying late or taking work home to get things done – only to be rewarded with more and more work. When eventually challenged by an anxious employee, the boss accuses them of being poor at time management! 'You must learn to manage your time better,' is the nagging phrase I often hear.

If you are an employee suffering from this situation, you should know that *it isn't always you to blame*! I know people who are very good at managing their time at work, yet still get into time trouble. Sometimes the blame belongs to the boss. There are a set number of hours available and even a trainee Time Master can only do so much.

If you have such a boss, then one of the things you can seek to do is to reverse the roles and manage your boss when it comes to time-related issues.

Here are a few tips for educating, training and managing your boss into better time management skills.

TIME MASTER TIPS TO MANAGE YOUR BOSS

HAVE THE COURAGE TO DISCUSS TIME MANAGEMENT ISSUES WITH YOUR BOSS

Nobody else needs to know of your discussion. Many people complain about the unreasonable demands their boss places on them but don't have the courage to discuss this politely and professionally. I have encountered many situations when the boss has genuinely been upset and apologetic when told of the problem, not having appreciated the problems they were causing.

DON'T BE AFRAID TO ASK YOUR BOSS ABOUT PRIORITIES

Actively make a point of exploring with your boss which of various activities has the highest priority. Apart from this being a useful guide for your own time management, it will educate and encourage your boss to start thinking in these terms.

TAKE ADVANTAGE OF OPPORTUNITIES TO PUT FORWARD SUGGESTIONS

As part of various internal schemes, employees are often asked to contribute ideas and suggestions. Don't hesitate to put forward ideas that will collectively benefit your time control. Obviously, you shouldn't draft this as an open criticism of your boss. You should make some general positive suggestions for the benefit of everyone that may make your boss rethink certain issues.

ASK FOR HELP FROM ABOVE

No, I am not suggesting divine intervention, although perhaps that might help. If you have tried everything else without success and the situation is not something you can live with on a long-term basis, you must speak to someone at a higher level within the company. If others feel the same then involve them too. If there is no higher level, you may need to balance out the benefits against the stresses of staying.

GET TO KNOW YOUR BOSS BETTER

Many people go out of their way to avoid the boss – consider doing the opposite. Speak to them, ask about their weekends and holidays. The better you know the person, the more chance you have of being able to influence them. Likewise, the better they know you, the more likely they are to see you as a real person and not just someone at their command.

RAISE ISSUES PRIOR TO MEETINGS

Meetings can be a major problem area, with a disproportionate amount of time spent talking about things that are not critical. These often take you away from doing the job itself. If you flag up other commitments you have and provide a suggested list of things you would like to see on the agenda, it might affect and minimize how long meetings take. Similarly, you might be able to suggest something that does away with the need for a meeting altogether.

LEARN TO SAY 'NO' PROPERLY

Sometimes the problem is partly caused by *you* agreeing all the time to every demand. If you foster this expectation, don't be surprised if you keep being given more to do.

While I recognize that saying 'no' to your boss may be hard and test your courage and diplomatic skills, there will be times you need to do so. The key is always to give a response with a good reason. A 'yes but' answer is often very helpful. Try to suggest that you are putting your employer's interests first, or that you are being respectful and honourable to an important existing personal commitment. Most reasonable people will respect your openness. It is also a good strategy to invite your boss to share in the prioritization process.

Your aim is to create the impression that you have thought things through properly and that you are not just saying 'no' because you are lazy or inefficient. The other thing you should factor into your thinking is that there may be times when your immediate line manager is unaware of tasks that someone else has given to you. With that in mind, here are a few suggestions for creative adaptations.

Six ways to say 'no' to your boss

- 'Sure, no problem, I can do that by 4 p.m. *but* I'll have to let something else go if I am to meet your deadline. Is it important enough for me to do that?'
- 'Yes, I am happy to do that, *but* with everything else I have on at the moment I am not sure if I can do it justice. Is it okay if I take an extra couple of days to get it absolutely right?'
- 'Whoops, sounds like a priority clash to me. What do you want me to tackle first?'
- 'Do you mind if I pass it onto Bob? He is better placed to deal with this right now.'
- 'Forgive me for asking, but did you know that Janet has just given me a whole set of reports to work on by close of play today as well? Before I say 'yes' to too much, I'd really appreciate it if you could have a word with her first, to clarify which should get my immediate attention.'
- 'I can totally understand that it would be useful to go to that meeting on Saturday afternoon, *but* I've made an absolute promise to be at my daughter's swimming party at that time, so I'm really sorry, I just can't be there. Can we arrange the meeting for a better time?'

I know what you are thinking: What if my boss still presses me? My boss isn't reasonable. I want to be very clear. The above suggestions are just that, ideas that may help. Don't throw the towel in until you have tried everything. If your boss is an abusive, intimidating and unreasonable bully, then you may have no choice but to look elsewhere for work. Your choice to do so is still you taking control.

I have to be honest with you. In terms of time management, there is nothing more you can do but say 'no' respectfully and elegantly like a Time Master. Saying 'no' sometimes at least guarantees you more control than if you say 'yes' every time.

14

MASTER YOUR DELEGATION SKILLS

Delegation is a very simple solution for people who struggle to get things done and who perceive they have too much to do at any one time. It should be easy, but there are at least two problems, which is why it doesn't happen as often as it should.

First, for many people 'delegation' has been painted as a hugely complex business and an academic discipline in its own right. I have read so many jargon-filled articles that many ordinary folk struggling to cope could be forgiven for thinking that the science of delegation is simply beyond them. Secondly, many people are driven by the thought that by doing everything themselves they keep control of the task. In fact, in the context of managing time the exact opposite is usually true. Time Masters know that by hanging onto everything, in many cases they lose control of their time.

I want to set the record straight and take the mystique out of delegation. There is one simple Time Master question you need to ask yourself when virtually any task pops up, whether at work or home. Ready for it? Here it is:

Is there someone else who can do this better, faster, less expensively or at least as well as me?

You should print this question off in large bold print and hang it on your wall. Better still, why not get someone else to print and hang it for you!

If the answer is 'yes' for a particular task, then at the very least consider delegating. I have had many clients who clearly hadn't asked themselves this question.

One such client, a large legal practice, had one of its high-billing partners responsible for the firm's marketing. When I asked him why a marketing professional wasn't employed to do the job, I was told, 'We can't afford it.' I went on to discover through conversation with this partner that he had no training, experience or knowledge of marketing. He also confessed that it took him ages to carry out the simplest of tasks, which he admitted usually got poor results.

In addition to that, when we worked out the cost to the firm of him performing this role in lost chargeable hours, it was over three times the cost of employing a really experienced market-eer. Had he asked the key question above, he would have stood a chance of making the connection that getting someone else in would have been better, faster and less expensive!

I am well aware of the fact that I am choosing not to deal with the psychology of delegation, supervisory and management responsibilities, how to delegate and to whom. I am more interested in making you think about the question and the possibility of getting someone else to perform certain tasks for you, than I am in giving you definitive advice on delegation techniques. Once you have bought into the basic concept that this can help, you can subject yourself to other, more substantive reading material on the topic if you are interested.

Delegating is not merely a work- or office-related issue, there are many areas of your domestic and personal life where giving a job to someone else is appropriate. Use the same question at home: *'Is there someone else who can do this better, faster, less expensively or at least as well as me?'*

Could you, for example, benefit from someone to do your gardening, cleaning or ironing? Even simple things like making use of home delivery shopping from a supermarket are a form of delegation that can make a huge difference. If it saves one hour a week trekking around a supermarket, hauling things in and out of the trolley to the checkout, into the car, out of the car and into the house and then into the cupboards, you have gained just over two days in the year. If you have better things to do in that time, the cost of the delivery is a sound investment.

I do have one other simple Time Master tip to get you thinking about delegating more on every level. It is simple: go into holiday thinking mode. Pretend you are going away on holiday in a couple of weeks' time.

What are some of the things that occupy your mind? Well, you almost automatically think about delegation. You begin to channel your thinking into other ways of making things happen and getting things done while you are away.

At work you consider who will take your calls, go to your appointments, attend meetings, deal with clients and various projects. At home you explore who will look after your dog and water your plants. This is a good state of mind to be in throughout the year.

15

MASTER YOUR TIME-CHARGING

This short chapter is especially for business people who sell their time as part of their job or profession. You know who you are. Again, it is not a topic that is typically found in time management books or courses, but it is absolutely critical for many people. If you fail to control your time effectively and don't know how to manage the perception of your clients and customers towards 'time-charging', you are also allowing your revenue-generating function to be out of control. This is one of those situations where quite literally time is money.

Here are the major issues that business people ask me about:

- How do I deal with the 'how much?' question when I charge for the amount of time to be taken on a job or project?

- How do I charge enough when I know a job won't take that long?
- How do I control my time when people call me on the telephone for free advice?

DEALING WITH THE 'HOW MUCH?' QUESTION

Despite the fact that calls about what you charge represent potential business, I have encountered thousands of people who don't know how to deal with them effectively.

All too often such enquiries are dealt with very defensively and vaguely. The big problem for many people is that they charge for their time, but don't want to commit themselves straight off as they don't know how long a job or assignment might take. Ironically, this lack of clarity can be the very thing that puts potential customers off.

The other response I come across regularly from people who have to deal with these enquiries is the assumption that almost by definition, everyone who asks the price is a cheapskate who is only interested in the cost. This is what I call the 'price trap'. Enquiry handlers don't actually hear 'how much?', they mentally translate this into 'how cheap?' instead.

To get over these mental obstacles, here are a few simple tips.

INVITE CALLERS INTO A CONVERSATION TO GET BACKGROUND

When someone launches into, 'Can you give me an indication of how much?' simply respond positively with something like:

'No problem, I'm more than happy to give you an indication of likely charges. Can I just check you are okay for a few minutes so that I can get a bit more background about what you are looking for, your personal circumstances and so on? What I need to do is get an understanding of how much time is likely to be involved so that I can be as helpful as possible over our charges. Is that okay?'

ADD A PERCENTAGE TO YOUR ESTIMATE AND GIVE A BALLPARK FIGURE

Once you have a grasp of the caller's requirements or you have met them and looked over the possible job, your own experience of similar work ought to give you a high percentage likelihood of getting your time estimate right. For safety, however, you should add on a small percentage increase as insurance in case you are wrong, and say to your potential client or customer:

'I understand you need to feel relaxed over our charging on this, but I'm also sure you can appreciate that it is difficult for us to be exact at this stage about how much time is going to be involved. So how about we do this? From the information you have given me and from what I can see, if I were to say that my charges to help you with this will be between £x and £y, does that make you feel reasonably comfortable? If it turns out from the amount of time put in that it is more than £y, that is all I will charge; if it works out that it require less time, I will give you the benefit of that and charge you at the lower end of the scale.'

This is a summarized version of how to deal with this problem, which works around 80% of the time. The reason it is so successful is that most people are risk averse when it comes to charging by time. This sort of approach gives them a degree of certainty and a sense of control that their interests are being protected. It also helps that they know you understand the situation from their perspective.

From your point of view as the supplier, this approach maximizes the potential of being paid appropriately for your time.

CHARGING ENOUGH WHEN A JOB DOESN'T TAKE THAT LONG

When you are considering your charges, make sure that they reflect the value to your potential client or customer and not just the actual time taken. Let me tell you a simple story to illustrate the point.

A man was driving home one night when his car broke down. A passing mechanic stopped and offered to try to get it going again for a fee. After gazing at the engine for just 30 seconds, he banged once on the front of the car with his fist. He invited the man to get in and try the engine. Amazingly, it started first time.

'Fantastic,' the man said, 'how much do I owe you?'

'£25,' replied the mechanic.

'£25 for one bang on the car? That's ridiculous!' said the man.

'No,' replied the mechanic, 'for the bang on the car I only charge £1, but for knowing where to bang I charge £24.'

Remember, however much time it takes you to perform a task, the real value a potential client or customer gets is that your time investment over the years has taught you where to bang! You should be charging for that too.

CONTROLLING YOUR TIME WHEN PEOPLE CALL FOR FREE ADVICE

People often complain, 'I find myself sucked into a half-hour conversation, giving free advice and then get nothing in return. This can happen several times a day.'

What do you do when potential clients and customers appear to be after your time for free advice over the phone? Here are a few tips.

DON'T FALL INTO THE 'FREE ADVICE' TRAP

Don't make the assumption at the beginning of the conversation that the caller is only after free advice and that they are offering you no prospect of business. Be prepared to invest some time before you make that judgement.

TAKE CONTROL AND SOW SEEDS ABOUT CHARGING FOR YOUR TIME AT THE OUTSET

This is very much the key to this situation. The longer you allow the caller to control the conversation, the more you will get sucked into spending your time giving free advice. You need to strike a balance between giving a good service, being interested in the caller, yet remaining commercially astute and in control over your own time. Try something like this:

'I am more than happy to listen for a while to get a grasp of your situation and what you need. Just to explain, however, I am okay for 10 minutes or so at the moment without any cost at all, to identify whether this is something we can definitely help you with. Obviously, you also need to decide if you are comfortable with us as well. By the time we've chatted for a while, I'll have a good feel for whether we should move forward on this straight away, whether we need to meet so I can get more details, or whether I should pass altogether. If it is either of the first two, we'll obviously need to find a financial arrangement that is acceptable to you. Is it okay to chat on that basis?'

16

MASTER YOUR DECISION-MAKING

How much time do you spend making decisions? Are you guilty of paralysis by analysis? Believe it or not, something that often soaks up a disproportionate amount of time is procrastinating over making decisions, which may not even be about huge, life-changing issues.

Some people can spend ages on relatively trivial and domestic decision-making. For example, I know people who will put off booking a holiday until they have researched every hotel in every resort, read every review, studied the weather forecasts and statistics for that time of the year, compared the prices of every operator and the reliability of the airlines. Finally, what do they book? Absolutely nothing, because the more information they have gathered, the more confused they get and the more negatives they have about everything. I have seen the same happen with choosing clothes, fountain pens, cars or even selecting what to eat from a menu.

Worse still, if the decision to be made is over something really major, then the time spent feeling anxious and coming to a conclusion can be even longer. I have seen people lose hours of their time worrying, thinking and discussing possible outcomes. Their time is out of control until a decision is made. This is a Time Master issue: how can you master your thinking in this sort of situation to control and minimize the amount of time spent?

As a starting point, you need to consider:

- How much of your time you are willing to give up to make a decision.
- What else you could be doing with that time.
- That there isn't always a right answer!
- That sometimes it really doesn't matter, there are no long-term consequences.
- That you need to ask yourself the right questions to reach a good decision.

TIME MASTER QUESTIONS TO ASK YOURSELF WHEN MAKING DECISIONS

The key to effective and time proportionate decision-making is the quality of the questions you ask yourself. Hopefully, the questions below should act as a powerful stimulus to help you look at things in a way that triggers the right decision for you.

WHAT FEELS RIGHT?

One of the great causes of stress in decision-making situations is the notion that there really is an absolutely right decision, that if you talk, think, debate and beat yourself up long and hard enough you will eventually arrive at an answer that leaves no room for doubt.

The truth is that decision-making is not an exact science: sometimes you have to proceed with confidence one way or the other based on what feels right. If this is a bit too vague for you, try a different question. Ask it out loud and answer with your gut feel and conscience, regardless of whether your response seems logical or not. The question is: Which route instinctively gives me the most peace of mind?

Learn to listen to the answer. Regardless of how you label it, common sense, divine intervention, self-doubt, I try to listen very carefully to that mysterious voice of reason in my head and act on it!

WHAT IF I MAKE THE WRONG DECISION?

I have often been in situations where people are asking my advice when they are not sure what to do. When I suggest one course of action, they respond, 'Yes, but what if such and such a thing were to happen?' 'Okay then, what about the other option?' I might respond. The answer I regularly get back is 'Well, I can't do that either because what if...?' Now they have ruled out both choices by playing the 'what if?' game.

When you get to this sort of 'thought block', try these questions to clear your thinking. If you *were* to get it wrong:

- What would the worst consequences be?
- Could you live with these consequences?
- At that time could you change your mind or revert to an acceptable alternative?

If you knew that even if the decision went wrong there was a decent alternative, or if not you could still live with whatever the consequences were, then you may have the courage to go along with your instinct instead of fearing your own personal 'what if?'.

Along with these questions you should also ask, if you got it *right*:

- What is the very best that could happen?

Now ask yourself: do the potential benefits of your decision outweigh the possible negative consequences of getting it wrong?

IF OTHER PEOPLE ARE INVOLVED, DO I HAVE DOUBTS ABOUT THEM?

There will be occasions when your decision really comes down to the people you might be dealing with if you choose a particular course of action. Someone may have made you a business proposal that seemed fantastic, or on a personal level someone has invited you to do something with them, and you have to decide 'yes' or 'no'.

Answer these questions honestly with either 'yes', 'no' or 'have doubts':

- Am I going to be able to get on with this person in the future?
- Do we have shared values?
- Do I feel comfortable around this person?
- Do I respect this person?

If you have answered 'yes' to all four, then don't hesitate to say 'yes' to the offer or invitation if the practical details are attractive. If you have said 'no' or 'have doubts' to any of them, perhaps this will trigger a 'that's it' moment for you and you'll turn the deal down or decline the invitation.

WHAT IS YOUR DECISION-MAKING TRACK RECORD?

Given that in most circumstances there isn't a definite right or wrong, most mere mortals make decisions hoping that we get it right more often than we get it wrong.

With this in mind, analyse your decision-making track record. Identify the last 10 really important decisions you have had to make; go back over the years if you have to and take your time. For example:

- Should I do that course or not?
- Which of these two new products should we launch first?
- Should we move to a new city?

- Should we increase our fees or not?
- Should we buy a second home as an investment?
- Should I accept that job or stay where I am?
- Should I go it alone and start my own business?

When you have written down your own list, ask yourself what your track record is of making the right decision. If you have a high success rate, then you ought to be able to trust your judgement with confidence and maximum peace of mind.

At the end of the day, don't spend a disproportionate amount of time making your mind up over things. Avoid being controlled by 'what if?' and your fear of being wrong.

17

MASTER YOUR HEALTH

Here's a curious thing. Look in any general book on healthy living and you will usually find a section on stress and the need to control, plan and organize your time better to avoid physical and mental overload. But have a flick through the leading time management books and guess what? You'll be hard pushed to find anything on health.

I am not a healthy living or exercise expert, but my role in raising this is simply because I want to help you join the dots to make a psychological connection between health and time management.

The reason is very simple. If you don't make time now to maximize your health, you may find yourself having no choice but to find time tomorrow for being ill and having health problems.

Of course, nobody is immune to being ill, but there are things you can do as far as your time planning is concerned to minimize health-related problems.

MAKE TIME FOR EXERCISE

People make two main excuses for not exercising regularly: 'I just don't have time,' and 'I don't enjoy exercising.'

So far as the first excuse is concerned, remember that people who exercise still have the same amount of hours in the day available to them as people who are inactive. The fact that you are a super-busy, important executive doesn't mean that you have less time. Some of the world's top leaders in politics and business understand the benefits of keeping fit and they *make* time for it. They know that it enhances their ability to get their job done.

Ultimately, it is merely a matter of priorities and planning. The Time Master way is to put yourself first in the time planning process. With this philosophy in mind, the first planning question becomes: 'How and when can I *make* time to exercise?' All too often people plan all their professional commitments first, only to find that there is nothing left for themselves.

To the 'I don't enjoy exercise' brigade, the answer is easy. Find something that you *do* like. If the gym is not your thing, then walk a dog, try swimming, do some morning press-ups, play golf, buy a bike. If nothing gets your enthusiasm going, force yourself to park half a mile from your office and meetings and walk the last part, or choose to use the stairs and not the lift.

MAKE TIME TO THINK AND PLAN WHAT YOU EAT

Confession time again. I know virtually nothing about the field of nutrition. I do know, however, that people who eat junk food all the time and who don't make the time to think about and plan what they eat are more susceptible to health-related problems than people who do plan like this. If you want to be a healthy Time Master, make time to eat properly.

MAKE TIME TO SLEEP

There are many studies and reports available on the amount of sleep that is required. They cite different averages for various age groups and types of people. You instinctively know how much sleep you personally need to function at your most efficient. With this in mind, factor 'sleep time' into your personal time planning.

MAKE TIME TO GET THE RIGHT TOOLS

I have just returned from my second visit to an osteopath, with a third planned next week. Each session takes about two hours out of my schedule. My problem is ongoing neck and backache caused by sitting for too many hours in the wrong position writing this and other books or seminars. I now know, having taken the time at long last to find out, that my desk is too high and my office chair is useless. Apart from the discomfort and possible long-term damage, I am actually losing productive time by not having the right tools to do my job in the quickest and most comfortable way.

I am now practising what I preach and taking the time to discuss the purchase of a proper chair that is ergonomically sound for someone with my problems. I am also arranging to have an expert call to review my working position and set me up properly. All of this takes time and of course money, but it is better than being laid up and out of action for lengthy periods of time.

SEEK MEDICAL HELP AS SOON AS YOU ARE WORRIED ABOUT A PROBLEM

Take time out from your busy schedule and make it a priority to see a doctor, dentist or other relevant professional if you are having a health problem that is unusual for you or you are anxious about an ongoing health issue or something that is becoming intrusive. The sooner you make time for this, the less time you may need off work. In the worst-case scenario, making time to get checked out could literally be a life saver.

18

DON'T BE TIME BORED!

Every time management book I have ever seen looks exclusively at the problem of having too much to do in too little time. There is another huge personal time-related question that is never mentioned in these publications. What do you do when you have *too much* time on your hands and nothing to do? While I might not have all the answers, if you want to be a Time Master instead of being 'time bored' you need to consider and attempt to get control over this potential problem.

I have come across many people who say:

- 'I am retiring soon after 40 years of work and I haven't a clue what I am going to do with my time.'
- 'I sold my business six months ago and I'm bored out of my head.'
- 'My kids have just left home and I'm totally at a loose end.'

If you haven't reached this stage of life yet, here is a vital tip for you: it is equally important to manage, control and plan your time when you have plenty of it as it is when it seems to be in short supply.

A Google search for 'retirement planning' produced almost 22 million possible links, but not one of the first 100 deals with the issue of time planning during retirement years. Pretty much all of them focus exclusively on financial planning, pensions and tax. I find this bizarre. Consider too that I have seen statistics reporting that over 20% of the able-bodied retired population experience some level of depression and that boredom is one of the contributory factors.

As many as 60% of retiring people do not have a plan for what they will do and how they will spend their time after retirement.

What are your retirement plans? Remember, retirement is not an end in itself. I have seen people who count down the years and days until they retire. On day one of their retirement they are celebrating, but by the end of the first week they are wandering around their house fed up of watching daytime TV. The main ambition of a business friend of mine was to sell his business and retire on the proceeds. Six months after selling up, he was on pills and recovering from depression. His structure, personal significance, activity and purpose had gone, with nothing to replace it.

While I can't tell you precisely what to do, I can invite you to give some mental focus to the problem and explore some possibilities to reduce the chances of it happening.

The big problem many people face is that the question, 'What do I want to do in my retirement years?' is just too general. If any answers do suggest themselves they are also often so vague that they are not helpful at all: 'I just want to have the freedom to make choices,' or 'I'm looking forward to doing things I have never had the time to do,' or 'I want to travel.' These all sound good, but what exactly do they mean in day-to-day living when you really have nothing to do?

The Time Master way to find the answers is to narrow down the questions to specifics so that you can't help but come up with some specific and tangible possibilities to aim for.

To give you a helping hand and to show you what I mean, I'm going to give you a checklist. Go through these questions however far from or close to retirement you are. Run through the list once a year. In fact, why not plan when you will do it and make it a fun occasion? If you have someone close to you, a friend or family member, it can be a great dinner conversation to go through this together.

My checklist is not meant to be exhaustive, merely an indication of the process. I'm sure you can come up with other questions too. The only rule of this game is that you *must* have an answer. In making your list and having discussions, do not rule things out because you don't know *how* you could do them. The list is meant to be aspirational. In fact, working out the practical logistics is part of the process that will keep you busy.

YOUR TIME MASTER RETIREMENT CHECKLIST

Travel. If there was one place I haven't yet been to that I would like to visit in the future, where would it be?

Things. If there was one thing I could acquire, what would it be?

New experiences. If I could have a go at one thing that I have never tried, what would it be?

Knowledge. If I could learn more about any subject in particular, what would it be?

Skills. If I could develop one new skill that I don't possess, what would it be?

Job. If I was going to do some kind of paid work on a part-time basis, what would it be?

Past friendships. If there was one person from my past whom I would like to renew contact with, who would it be?

Helping. If there was one group or person I could support as a volunteer, who would it be?

Habits. If I could get rid of one bad habit of mine, what would it be?

Health. If there was one thing I could do that would help make me healthier or fitter, what would it be?

Have you got the hang of this yet? How many other questions like these can you come up with? Once you have the answers to these types of questions, go through each of them again with this set:

- What do I need to do to make it happen?
- When can it be done?
- What are the cost implications?
- How can I get the money?
- What are the steps I need to plan in and what are the priorities?

Merely making the time to go through this process constitutes recognition and acceptance of the problem. By doing so you are well on the way to turning these things into reality.

If you're now asked what you're going to do in your retirement years, at least you have an outline plan to work towards.

TIME MASTER TRAVEL TIPS

GET YOUR JOURNEY INFORMATION ONCE

A friend of mine operates like this. If he gets an invitation to travel somewhere on business, he looks at the train or travel times on the Internet, 'to see what sort of journey it's going to be'. Then a week or so before his journey and meeting he looks at the times again, this time 'to fix the details in my head', he says. Finally, two days before travelling, again he pulls up the train details on the web to book his tickets! On three separate occasions he has invested his time in doing battle with the train company's website; not an easy task. He could have done it once and dealt with all the issues then. How often do you replicate jobs unnecessarily?

ON HOLIDAY, TAKE OFF YOUR WATCH

How many times a day do you look at your watch? Are your days are governed and regulated by the information on your watch face?

One of the first things I do on holiday is to remove my watch and lock it away in the hotel safe. It is liberating not to know the time, so that how you feel controls what you do and when you do it, rather than living minute by minute according to your watch. Try it!

PLAN YOUR ROUTE

Have you ever got lost going to a meeting and arrived later than you would have liked? Those who know me well will smile at this tip. I get teased for my poor sense of direction: I can get lost on a train! To compensate for this, however, I always try to get detailed directions to where I am going, even when I am on foot, including landmarks I will be passing. I am sure I am not the only one who needs to do this!

AVOID THE WORST OF THE RUSH HOUR

This couldn't be more basic and obvious, yet most people don't do it. At one time I used to spend 40 minutes in a car every morning to drive seven miles to my office. If I left 10 minutes earlier, or even 30 minutes later, right at the tail end of the 'rush hour' period, I could do the journey in 15 minutes. Leave at a more 'time-sensible' time.

CHECK OUT OF HOTELS BEFORE BREAKFAST

Are you a regular visitor to hotels? How often have you stood at reception waiting to check out? Here is a really basic tip. As a hotel guest, I have often come down for breakfast early and walked past an empty reception desk, which will be busy once everyone has had breakfast, been back up and gathered their things together to leave. Do your checking out *before* breakfast, when nobody else is.

USE YOUR SAT-NAV

Some folk avoid using these fantastic machines: 'Oh, I know the way, I don't need to use the sat-nav.' It is not a sign of weakness to have one and to use it. It is foolish to risk getting lost and being late because you want to prove you are as smart as the device!

KEEP A BAG PACKED

If you travel regularly, keep a separate travel bag semi-ready with the things in it that you need with you every time you travel; separate toiletries, a stationery kit, medication and reading materials.

ACTIVELY USE YOUR DOWNTIME

How often do you sit on the train, bus or in your car on the way to work or on other journeys? Actively plan what you will do with your travel downtime. Take a book, a report you have been meaning to get around to reading or an empty notepad so that you can start that novel, update or draft your CV or listen to a CD.

SET YOUR WATCH THREE MINUTES FAST

This may seem a bit extreme and you might reasonably ask, 'Who are you kidding?' given that you are the one who has fixed it. The truth is that it does work. You will forget that the watch is three minutes fast and you will always have a few minutes in hand. This will prove very useful when catching trains and being up against a travel deadline.

GET READY IN GOOD TIME

Why wait until the last minute to get your things ready for your trip? Advance preparation means you can leave in good time, without stress, and minimizes the chance of forgetting something.

TRAVEL DIRECT

Whenever you can, minimize the connections you have to make on a journey. The more connections there are, the greater the waiting time and the higher the risk of unexpected delays.

INVEST IN QUEUE-JUMPING OFFERS

If you are travelling by air, there are now various options for paying a nominal extra fee that allows you into a special security queue, which speeds up the process. Some airlines also give you the possibility of jumping the main check-in queues and boarding the aircraft first. If you can afford to pay, do so.

BOOK IN ADVANCE

Suppose you are on a short city break or holiday and you want to visit an important tourist attraction. Whenever you can, book your tickets beforehand. This could save you hours of queuing when you get there.

TIME MASTER SHOPPING TIPS

MAKE SURE THE SHOP IS OPEN

Visit the store's website or call if you have any doubt at all about opening hours.

HAVE A SHOPPING LIST

Have you ever been to the shops, got home and unpacked your bags, only to realize that you forgot something important? Have a shopping list in your kitchen that stays in the same place all the time, with a pen next to it that lives there too. The moment you run out of something, write it on the list.

KEEP A SUPERMARKET COIN

Ever got to the supermarket and realized you don't have a pound coin for the trolley and spent time having to get change? Solve the problem today: get one of those trolley tokens that stays on your key ring. You'll never have the problem again!

SHOP WHEN OTHER PEOPLE AREN'T THERE

Shop in the evenings when shops are least busy. Consider doing much of your Christmas shopping in January when it is quieter, quicker and cheaper.

> Just 15 minutes of queuing in supermarkets, shops, banks and so on three times a week = 1.62 days a year.

DON'T BE A CHECKOUT SHEEP

Have you ever been in the supermarket or another type of shop, picked up three items and then had to wait in the checkout behind people with a full trolley or in the express lane behind 10 people also with a few items. Consider taking your things elsewhere to pay, for example to the newsagent section, customer service desk or a different department. I have regularly cut 20 minutes' checkout queuing down to a minute by taking certain food or hardware items from the downstairs to the upstairs section of my local supermarket, where they mainly sell clothes and electrical products.

CHECK PRICES BEFORE YOU GO SHOPPING

I know people who will spend a day trekking from shop to shop to find out the price of certain items they already know they want to buy. If you enjoy this and you have the time, that's fine.

If you want to be more time efficient, then telephone the stores in advance to find out their prices or use specific store or comparison websites.

SHOP ONLINE WITH HOME DELIVERY

This is very common these days. Browse the Internet, visit the store's website, pop your choices into the virtual trolley or basket, pay with your card and allow the company to deliver to your doorstep. This can save a huge amount of time.

CHECK WHETHER ITEMS ARE IN STOCK BEFORE YOU GO SHOPPING

Have you ever gone out to buy a particular item, only to discover when you get there that they don't have your size or the colour you want? Call the store before you go to check they have exactly what you want and even have them put it on one side for you.

IF YOU ARE SHOPPING FOR OTHERS, KNOW EXACTLY WHAT THEY WANT

Have you ever shopped for other people? If so, go through the shopping list with them before you set off to get clarity on exactly what they mean. In this day and age of huge choice, it is not helpful or time efficient to see the phrase 'biscuits' or 'ice cream' on the list without being more specific.

TIME MASTER EATING OUT TIPS

ONLY GO TO RESTAURANTS THAT TAKE BOOKINGS

Have you ever walked into a restaurant and been told you have a 50-minute wait for a table? You are now faced with the decision of waiting or going elsewhere. This is an easy problem. Where time is an issue, only eat in restaurants that take bookings and book as soon as you can.

STUDY THE MENU ONLINE

Many restaurants have their menus online. Why not decide what you want before you go so that you can order almost straight away?

CHECK THAT THE RESTAURANT IS OPEN

Many restaurants have days when they are closed and variable opening hours. Do your homework before setting off. You don't want to spend time outside a closed place deciding, 'Where now?'

ORDER STRAIGHT AWAY

How often have you been to a restaurant and had to wait longer than you wanted to give your order? Here is what you do to get your food as fast as possible. As soon as you have been seated and handed your menus, say to the waiting staff, 'Don't go, we'll order now when you're here.' In most cases, even if you take a while they will wait for you to choose.

ASK FOR THE BILL BEFORE YOU'RE READY TO LEAVE

Have you ever finished your meal, chatted for a while and then had to wait ages for staff to bring your bill? As soon as you have got to the stage where you know you are not ordering anything else, ask for and even pay the bill.

TIME MASTER BUSINESS TIPS

TIME SENDING YOUR BILL FOR THE PEAK OF THE GRATITUDE CURVE

If you have done a job for someone, provided a service or supplied goods, invoice them as soon as you can. The best time is when they are most grateful.

IF YOU'RE IN SALES, KNOW WHEN TO STOP CHASING!

I have encountered many sales people who know that following up leads is important, yet throw a disproportionate amount of time at chasing what I would regard as dead leads. If after three attempted follow-up contacts you don't hear back from someone, simply move on. Use your valuable time in a more productive way.

ALWAYS CONFIRM YOUR MEETINGS

Have you ever had a misunderstanding over the time, date or venue of a meeting, leaving you hanging around waiting, rushing to another venue or discovering you have no meeting at all? If possible, double-check with the person concerned before leaving home or work for the meeting.

TRY TO COORDINATE MEETINGS

If I have to travel some distance for a business engagement, I always consider what else I can usefully do while in that general area. Often I find I am able to coordinate two or three meetings for the same away and travel time, making it all much more time efficient.

LEARN THE RIGHT SKILLS

I recently spoke to the director of an organization who was worried about the amount of lost time involved in attending sales meetings that were not successful. He and his team had about 150 face-to-face sales meetings a year, with only a 10% success rate. He admitted that none of his people who attended these meetings had any sales training or experience. Make sure that you or your team have the necessary skills to do the job in the most successful and time-efficient way.

AVOID LITIGATION

Factor in the time drain on your resources as well as the monetary implications.

BE KIND TO YOURSELF WHEN COMMITTING TO DEADLINES

Have you ever been in a situation when a client, customer, business contact or even your boss says, 'So when can you do that by?' Do you ever hear your voice agreeing to a particular time scale, but then listen to your brain telling you, 'You moron, why did you just promise that, how on earth is that possible?' Be sensible and don't put yourself in a no-win situation, where if you don't meet the deadline you look bad, but if you do it is only because you have paid a price for it in terms of stress and not doing other things. The trick is to underpromise and then aim to overdeliver.

WORK AT HOME IF POSSIBLE

Working at home is on the increase and rightly so. People spend a disproportionate amount of time travelling to an office to sit at a desk, work on a computer or talk to people on the phone. Wherever possible explore working from home, but plan what you will do and set yourself up properly to minimize disruptions.

TIME MASTER NETWORKING TIPS

Networking usually doesn't feature in time management books. I'll tell you why it appears in mine. After years of advising commercial organizations of various types and their professional personnel, I remain convinced that building contacts with others and tapping into their know-how saves huge amounts of time. Why spend time trying to open doors when you can get others to open them for you?

> People worldwide collectively spend a whopping 2.6 billion minutes on social networking sites like Facebook every day.

CONVERT YOUR TIME INTO MONEY

How much is your time at work worth? Ever worked it out? As a very rough guide, divide your annual salary by 2000. This will give you an indication of the cost to your organization of each hour of your time. Better still, divide by 120000 and you'll even have the cost per minute.

LEARN TO INVEST SPECULATIVE TIME WISELY

In my capacity as a consultant and presenter, I often get asked, 'Is it worth the time and money to go to such and such a networking meeting or event?' Subject to the cost and potential benefits being proportionate, my answer is usually, 'If you don't go, you'll never know.' Build in time throughout your year for totally speculative things and learn the skills to take advantage of whatever these events or opportunities are.

Make sure that you plan them properly, however. Know what you will do when you get there and who you want to meet, and plan into your system time to do the follow-up that will definitely be required.

THE TIME MASTER COMMANDMENTS

PRACTICE THE 'WWW QUESTION' APPROACH TO PLANNING

W = *What* do you have to and want to get done?

W = *When* exactly will you do it?

W = *Where* will you write this information down so that it is easily visible and accessible to remind you?

DO THE MOST IMPORTANT THING FIRST

Ask yourself: 'What is the most important thing to do first?' Once you have an answer, that is what you should do. Once that is done, you move to the next most important task.

UNDERSTAND THE DIFFERENCE BETWEEN PROCRASTINATION AND PRIORITIZATION

Sometimes it is sensible to put things off because of a conscious decision that something else is more important at that time.

When you do this, however, plan when you will do whatever you have put off.

BREAK ALL TASKS OR PROJECTS INTO BITS!

Don't start any job until you have broken it up into a series of smaller tasks and prioritized them.

PUT YOURSELF AND YOUR FAMILY FIRST WHEN IT COMES TO PLANNING

Don't just allow yourself the time left over after everything else. Build your plan and life around the personal things you want to do.

LEARN TO SAY 'NO'

You don't have to say 'yes' to every request or interruption. Develop the courage and skill to say 'no' when you want to.

TURN YOUR GADGETS OFF

It is okay turn off your email, mobile phone and pager and to screen your phone calls. Time Masters know that they don't have to be on call 24 hours a day.

STOP THINKING IN HALF-HOUR OR HOUR TIME SLOTS

Your days don't have to revolve around whole-hour and half-hour time slots. By thinking outside of these, you can create more time frames and options for yourself.

DON'T GET TRAPPED BY 'SUNK TIME'

What you have done in the past doesn't justify doing things in the future that you don't want! Regardless of future outcomes, your time has already gone.

STOPPING AND RELAXING IS NOT A WASTE OF TIME

It is often in these moments that important and innovative ideas take shape and the most significant and wisest decisions are made.

DON'T KEEP YOUR 'TO DO' LIST IN YOUR HEAD

Have a habit and system of writing down the things you have to do and storing them so that they are easily accessible in the future.

PLAN FOR HAVING TOO MUCH TIME

When you have plenty of it, as it is when it seems to be in short supply. Plan ahead for your time when thinking about your retirement years or even just the weekends.

SET TARGETS AND REWARD YOURSELF

If you have just performed an organizational task that you have been putting off, reward yourself. Look forward to the reward as well.

TIME MASTERS ARE ONLY HUMAN!

However good you get at managing your time and however hard you try, things will crop up to throw you off course. Accept this as a fact of life and being human. However, you should not allow these challenges to tarnish your efforts and make you feel like a time management failure. Just smile at them, learn from them and carry on!

"Yesterday is history. Tomorrow is a mystery. And today? Today is a gift. That's why we call it the present."

Babatunde Olatunji

INDEX